John Bunyan

John Bunyan (1628–1688)

(picture courtesy of David Lachman)

"Venture All for God"

Piety in the Writings of John Bunyan

Introduced and Edited by
Roger D. Duke and Phil A. Newton
with Drew Harris

Reformation Heritage Books
Grand Rapids, Michigan

"Venture All for God"
© 2011 by Roger D. Duke and Phil A. Newton

Published by
Reformation Heritage Books
2965 Leonard St. NE
Grand Rapids, MI 49525
616-977-0889/Fax: 616-285-3246
e-mail: orders@heritagebooks.org
website: www.heritagebooks.org

All rights reserved. No part of this book may be reproduced, stored in a retrieval system, or transmitted in any form or by any means—electronic, mechanical, photocopying, recording, or otherwise—except for brief quotations for the purpose of review or comment, without the prior permission of the publisher, Reformation Heritage Books.

Printed in the United States of America
11 12 13 14 15 16/10 9 8 7 6 5 4 3 2 1

Library of Congress Cataloging-in-Publication Data

Bunyan, John, 1628-1688.
 "Venture all for God" : piety in the writings of John Bunyan / John Bunyan ; introduced and edited by Roger D. Duke and Phil A. Newton with Drew Harris.
  p. cm. — (Profiles in Reformed spirituality)
 ISBN 978-1-60178-153-6 (pbk. : alk. paper)
 1. Christian literature, English—History and criticism. 2. Theology—Early works to 1800. I. Duke, Roger D. II. Newton, Phil A. III. Harris, Drew L. IV. Title.
 BR75.B865 2011
 230'.58—dc23
                                    2011037629

For additional Reformed literature, both new and used, request a free book list from Reformation Heritage Books at the above address.

For unceasing support of the
gospel and our ministries,
we lovingly dedicate this book to our wives,
Linda Duke and Karen Newton.
—ROGER DUKE AND PHIL NEWTON

For encouragement and love as we
begin our pilgrimage in Christ together,
I lovingly dedicate this book to
my wife, Jenny Harris.
—DREW HARRIS

PROFILES IN REFORMED SPIRITUALITY
series editors—Joel R. Beeke and Michael A. G. Haykin

Other Books in the Series:
Michael Haykin, *"A Consuming Fire": The Piety of Alexander Whyte of Free St. George's*

Michael Haykin, *"A Sweet Flame": Piety in the Letters of Jonathan Edwards*

Michael Haykin and Steve Weaver, *"Devoted to the Service of the Temple": Piety, Persecution, and Ministry in the Writings of Hercules Collins*

Michael Haykin and Darrin R. Brooker, *"Christ Is All": The Piety of Horatius Bonar*

J. Stephen Yuille, *"Trading and Thriving in Godliness": The Piety of George Swinnock*

Joel R. Beeke, *"The Soul of Life": The Piety of John Calvin*

Thabiti Anyabwile, *"May We Meet in the Heavenly World": The Piety of Lemuel Haynes*

Joel R. Beeke and Mark Jones, *"A Habitual Sight of Him": The Christ-Centered Piety of Thomas Goodwin*

Matthew Vogan, *"The King in His Beauty": The Piety of Samuel Rutherford*

James M. Garretson, *"A Scribe Well-Trained": Archibald Alexander and the Life of Piety*

Table of Contents

Profiles in Reformed Spirituality xi
Preface xv
The Piety of John Bunyan (1628–1688) 1

Section One: Christ Our Advocate

1. Advantages and Privileges for Those Who
   Have Jesus Christ as Advocate 59
2. The Physician Who Cures Gets Himself
   a Name and Begets Encouragement in
   the Minds of Diseased Folk 63
3. Things Related to the Promises of Christ
   Our Advocate 67
4. Concerning Christ's Sacrifice 72
5. Concerning Eternal Security 74
6. Concerning Christ's Blood—Our Only Plea . . . 76

Section Two: Christ Jesus the Merciful Savior

7. Christ's Mercy Offered to the Biggest Sinners
   Redounds Most to the Fame of His Name 81
8. Christ's Offer of Mercy 85
9. Encouragement to the Unbeliever Not
   to Despair 88

10. Mercy Offered to All Sinners—
    Great or Small! 93
11. What Is Meant by This "Water of Life"? 97

Section Three: Hope for Sinners

12. A Great Sinner's Encouragement
    to Come to Christ 103
13. Biggest Sinners Have the Most
    Need of Mercy 107
14. God's "Bending" of Men's Hearts 111
15. Born of God: A Sermon on John 1:13 115
16. The Excellence of a Broken Heart
    before God 119
17. The Questioning Soul 123
18. A Contrite Heart before God 128

Section Four: True Humility

19. Four Things That Are Acceptable to God ... 133
20. The Evil Effects of the Sin of Pride 134
21. Some Signs of a Broken Heart, of a
    Broken and Contrite Spirit 138

Section Five: Christian Ethics

22. A Simple Christian's View of Extortion 143
23. Instructions for Righteous Trading 146
24. Strictures against Fraudulent Bankruptcy .. 150

Section Six: The Gospel Applied

25. What It Is to Be Offered 157
26. Prison Meditations 162

Section Seven: Warnings

27. God Would Show the Greatness of His
    Anger against Sin and Sinners. 171
28. Reasons or Causes for Pride 175
29. Of the Unchangeableness of Eternal
    Reprobation 178
30. Warning to False Professors of Religion 182
31. Without Godly Repentance, the Wicked
    Man's Hope and Life Die Together 186

Reading Bunyan 191

Profiles in Reformed Spirituality

Charles Dickens's famous line in *A Tale of Two Cities*—"It was the best of times, it was the worst of times"—seems well suited to western evangelicalism since the 1960s. On the one hand, these decades have seen much for which to praise God and to rejoice. In His goodness and grace, for instance, Reformed truth is no longer a house under siege. Growing numbers identify themselves theologically with what we hold to be biblical truth, namely, Reformed theology and piety. And yet, as an increasing number of Reformed authors have noted, there are many sectors of the surrounding western evangelicalism that are characterized by great shallowness and a trivialization of the weighty things of God. So much of evangelical worship seems barren. And when it comes to spirituality, there is little evidence of the riches of our heritage as Reformed evangelicals.

As it was at the time of the Reformation, when the watchword was *ad fontes*—"back to the sources"—so it is now: The way forward is backward. We need to go back to the spiritual heritage of Reformed evangelicalism to find the pathway forward. We cannot live in the past; to attempt to do so would be antiquarianism. But our Reformed forebearers in the faith can teach us much about Christianity, its doctrines, its passions, and its fruit.

And they can serve as our role models. As R. C. Sproul has noted of such giants as Augustine, Martin Luther, John Calvin, and Jonathan Edwards: "These men all were conquered, overwhelmed, and spiritually intoxicated by their vision of the holiness of God. Their minds and imaginations were captured by the majesty of God the Father. Each of them possessed a profound affection for the sweetness and excellence of Christ. There was in each of them a singular and unswerving loyalty to Christ that spoke of a citizenship in heaven that was always more precious to them than the applause of men."[1]

To be sure, we would not dream of placing these men and their writings alongside the Word of God. John Jewel (1522–1571), the Anglican apologist, once stated: "What say we of the fathers, Augustine, Ambrose, Jerome, Cyprian?… They were learned men, and learned fathers; the instruments of the mercy of God, and vessels full of grace. We despise them not, we read them, we reverence them, and give thanks unto God for them. Yet…we may not make them the foundation and warrant of our conscience: we may not put our trust in them. Our trust is in the name of the Lord."[2]

Seeking, then, both to honor the past and yet not idolize it, we are issuing these books in the series Profiles in Reformed Spirituality. The design is to introduce the spirituality and piety of the Reformed

---

1. R. C. Sproul, "An Invaluable Heritage," *Tabletalk* 23, no. 10 (October 1999): 5–6.

2. Cited in Barrington R. White, "Why Bother with History?" *Baptist History and Heritage* 4, no. 2 (July 1969): 85.

tradition by presenting descriptions of the lives of notable Christians with select passages from their works. This combination of biographical sketches and collected portions from primary sources gives a taste of the subjects' contributions to our spiritual heritage and some direction as to how the reader can find further edification through their works. It is the hope of the publishers that this series will provide riches for those areas where we are poor and light of day where we are stumbling in the deepening twilight.

—Joel R. Beeke
Michael A. G. Haykin

Preface

Books come together in various ways. This book came out of the interesting work of providence in the editors' lives. Phil and Roger met over twenty years ago and kept in contact through conferences. Just a couple of years ago, Roger and his family became members of South Woods Baptist Church in Memphis, where Phil serves as senior pastor. Both Phil and Roger love books, church history, and theology and enjoy making a contribution to the church through writing. Discussion on book collaboration began to take shape when Roger spoke with noted Baptist historian Dr. Michael Haykin about putting together a book on John Bunyan. With Dr. Haykin's encouragement and Dr. Joel Beeke's positive response, this book on Bunyan's piety found life.

God's providence had prepared the writers for this challenge on Bunyan. In 2007, Phil was asked to give four lectures on John Bunyan for students of his alma mater, the University of Mobile. The Heritage Conference, sponsored by Lafitte Baptist Church of Saraland, Alabama, was well attended by enthusiastic collegians. During the summer of 2002, Roger provided a lecture in a doctoral class at the University of the South, an Episcopal university, on the significant Baptist father John Bunyan. The two events resulted in manuscripts on John Bunyan waiting for a place to land. But without some significant editorial work to put them together, that could not happen.

Drew Harris began attending South Woods shortly after Roger and his family joined. While participating in a pastoral internship program, Drew did a book review for the rest of the interns. His skill in synthesizing and evaluating his assigned book demonstrated superb journalistic gifts. When Phil and Roger began discussing the possibility of putting their manuscripts together into a book addressing John Bunyan's life and piety, Drew immediately came to mind as the one with the gifts to bring it about.

John Bunyan speaks for himself. The editors' task (and a joyous one at that) has been to simply let Bunyan speak, and in doing so, to encourage believers to "venture all for God." As much as that has been accomplished, the editors give thanks to the Lord.

Note of interest: The image used at the end of most selections is one of the three bronze panels on the pedestal of the John Bunyan statue in Bedford, England. Each panel depicts a scene from *Pilgrim's Progress*. The one used here portrays Christian's meeting with Evangelist.

I had also this consideration, that if I should now venture all for God, I engaged God to take care of my concernments; but if I forsook him and his ways, for fear of any trouble that should come to me or mine, then I should not only falsify my profession, but should count also that my concernments were not so sure, if left at God's feet, while I stood to and for his name, as they would be, if they were under my own [care].

—John Bunyan

John Bunyan

The Piety of John Bunyan (1628–1688)

John Bunyan ventured all for God in the face of immeasurable religious and political upheaval. For a century before his birth and throughout his lifetime, England was in continual turmoil as the country vacillated between monarchical and parliamentarian government. Intertwined with this struggle for power were the competing interests of Roman Catholicism, the Church of England, and Protestant Separatists. This historical milieu of political unrest and religious persecution by the English government provides a necessary framework for understanding the life and works of Bunyan. Bunyan's persecution and imprisonment shaped his own faith and personal piety, and the theme of Christian suffering reverberates in much of his writing.

During the English Reformation of the sixteenth century, Henry VIII (r. 1509–1547) sought legal accommodation to divorce Queen Catherine and marry Anne Boleyn. He enacted the 1534 Act of Supremacy that established the Church of England as distinct from the Roman Catholic Church. Henry became head of the church, with his reforms being primarily ecclesiological, not theological.[1] Under Edward VI, Henry's son, the communion cup was restored to the people, the clergy allowed to marry, images removed from the church, and the Book of Common Prayer (1549, 1552) published as the liturgical standard.[2] In 1549, Parliament passed the First Act of Uniformity coinciding with the publication of the Book of Common Prayer. It "abolished the Latin mass and made a new liturgy (the prayer book of 1549) the legal form of worship."[3] Though revolutionary for English citizens, this eventually proved to be a destructive act for the Puritans, including John Bunyan, whose imprisonment was the direct result of the First Act of Uniformity.

Mary I (r. 1553–1558) ascended the throne, reversing Protestant reforms and reestablishing Roman Catholicism as the state religion. She filled the Tower of London with Protestant prisoners and executed many whose stories were later recorded in John Foxe's *Book of Martyrs*. When Elizabeth I (r. 1558–1603) succeeded Mary I, she restored Anglicanism by the Second Act of Supremacy in 1559, declaring herself to be the governor of the church. The Second Act of Uniformity (1559) restored the liturgy of the Book of Common Prayer.[4] Elizabeth I was the last of the Tudor monarchy and was followed by Stuart

---

1. Stephen Nichols, *Pages from Church History: A Guided Tour of Christian Classics* (Phillipsburg, N.J.: P&R, 2006), 200–201.

2. Justo Gonzalez, *The Story of Christianity* (Peabody, Mass.: The Prince Press, 2001), 2:75–76.

3. Owen Chadwick, *The Penguin History of the Church: The Reformation* (New York: Penguin Books, 1972), 117–18.

4. Chadwick, *History of the Church*, 101, 132.

monarch James I (r. 1603–1625). His reign produced the colonization of the New World and the 1611 Authorized Version of the Bible. Charles I (r. 1625–1649) followed James I, and "with his reign the Reformation took a few steps back." His Catholic wife unduly influenced him, while his ineptness and inflexibility set him at odds with Parliament, laying the foundation for the English Civil War during the 1640s.[5]

Under Oliver Cromwell's leadership, parliamentary forces defeated King Charles's army in 1649 and then beheaded Charles later that year for high treason. Cromwell took the title of Lord Protector, leaving Britain without a monarchy. The monarchy was restored in 1660 under Charles II, and the period can be summed up as a time of "reaction against the Puritans."[6] This governmental crackdown was so harsh that none of the dissenting groups went unscathed. For Parliament and the general population, the persecution of a minority who was seen to cause political, religious, and social unrest was better than the whole nation being in turmoil.

With restoration of the episcopacy and the Book of Common Prayer, the achievements of the Puritans and Dissenters were reversed. In 1662, the Act of Uniformity forced all English ministers to believe and hold worship according to prescribed doctrines and liturgy. Those who did not conform were ejected from their positions. "This 'Great Ejection' saw about 20 percent of English clergy excluded,

---

5. Nichols, *Pages from Church History*, 205.
6. Gonzalez, *Story of Christianity*, 162.

including Presbyterians, Congregationalists, Independents, and about twenty Baptists who held livings put out."[7] The Conventicle Act in 1664 applied to Baptists like Bunyan most directly. "It set severe penalties for holding unauthorized worship services or 'conventicles' with more than five persons present beyond the immediate family. This did not prevent Baptists from meeting but did make their meetings more dangerous."[8]

Persecution continued during Charles II's reign, with his deathbed conversion to Roman Catholicism explaining much of the harsh treatment that Bunyan and other Puritans faced for nonconformity to the state religion. In 1689, a year after Bunyan's death, Prince William of Orange and Mary, daughter of James II, demonstrated tolerance in their coregency, highlighted by the 1689 Act of Toleration that granted religious freedom even to those not swearing allegiance to the Thirty-Nine Articles. Too late for Bunyan to enjoy, the door was opened for other Puritans and nonconformists to preach the gospel without encumbrance.

Early Years

John Bunyan was born November 30, 1628, to a moderate working-class family in the village of Elstow near Bedford and was baptized into the Church of England. Bunyan's father was a tinker, a mender of pots and other household utensils,

---

7. Leon McBeth, *The Baptist Heritage: Four Centuries of Witness* (Nashville: Broadman, 1987), 115.

8. McBeth, *Baptist Heritage*, 115.

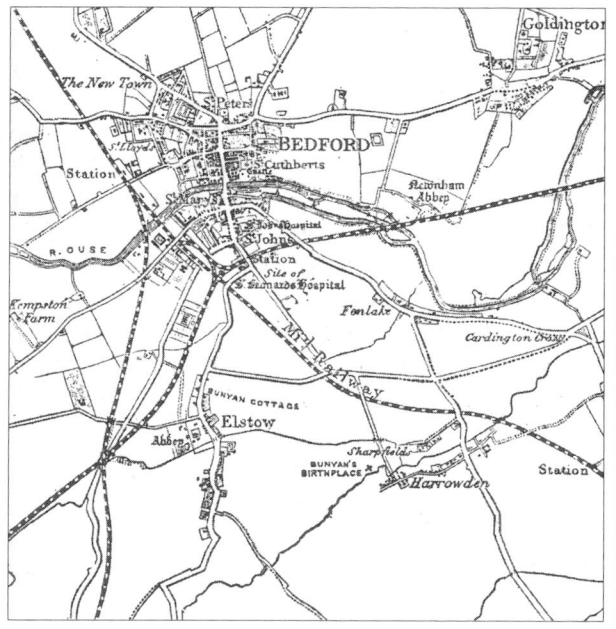

Map of Bedford and Elstow

Bunyan was born near the village of Elstow.
He moved to Bedford in 1655 and lived
there for the rest of his life.

and Bunyan followed his father in this profession. Bunyan's parents could not afford extensive formal education for their son, but in Bunyan's own words, "Notwithstanding the meanness and inconsiderableness of my Parents, it pleased God to put it into their heart, to put me to School, to learn both to Read and Write."[9]

Bunyan wrote virtually nothing about his parents, indicating their limited spiritual influence. He was not as reserved regarding his own spiritual condition as a boy and young man. He states in his autobiography, *Grace Abounding to the Chief of Sinners*, that from childhood he had few equals in personal ungodliness. He was given to "cursing, swearing, lying, and blaspheming the holy name of God," and throughout his teenage years, he had no thought of God, of piety, or of heaven and hell.[10] Though Bunyan accounted himself easily given to sin, he despised any religious hypocrite. If someone professed to be religious but didn't live the part, he said, "It would make my spirit tremble."[11] This attitude may have spurred his development of a wide array of hypocrites in his most famous work, *Pilgrim's Progress*, with such characters as Pliable, Presumption, Formalist, and Hypocrisy.

Despite his propensity toward sin and ungodliness, Bunyan later believed that God's sovereign

---

9. John Bunyan, *Grace Abounding to the Chief of Sinners*, in *The Works of John Bunyan*, ed. George Offor (1854; repr., Edinburgh: Banner of Truth, 1991), 1:6. All Bunyan quotations and extracts are taken from this three-volume edition of his works.

10. Bunyan, *Grace Abounding*, in *Works*, 1:6.

11. Bunyan, *Grace Abounding*, in *Works*, 1:7.

mercy protected him during his formative years. In *Grace Abounding*, he recalls how the Lord protected him in situations when he could have died. For example, in the English Civil War, he swapped guard duty with another soldier who was killed while serving on Bunyan's watch. Bunyan testified that "I with others were drawn to go to such a place to besiege it: but when I was just ready to go, one of the company desired to go in my room, to which, when I consented he took my place: and coming to the siege, as he stood sentinel, he was shot into the head with a musket bullett, and died."[12] This undoubtedly impacted Bunyan's piety and view of God's sovereignty.

In 1649, as a twenty-one-year-old, Bunyan married. Though no record exists of his first wife's name, he considered his marriage "an important turning point in his life."[13] Bunyan explained, "This woman and I, though we came together as poor as poor might be, not having so much household stuff as a dish or spoon betwixt us both, yet she had for her part, *The Plain Man's Pathway to Heaven* [Arthur Dent, 1601], and *The Practice of Piety* [Lewis Bayly, c. 1613], which her father had left her when he died."[14] Bunyan treasured the books and read them thoroughly. Although he was not yet spiritually awakened, he found inspiration in them to become religious.

---

12. Bunyan, *Grace Abounding*, in *Works*, 1:7.

13. David Calhoun, *Grace Abounding: The Life, Books and Influence of John Bunyan* (Fearn, Ross-shire, Scotland: Christian Focus Publications, 2005), 14.

14. Bunyan, *Grace Abounding*, in *Works*, 1:7.

Though not abandoning his wicked life, Bunyan began to attend church regularly and entered into the religious superstitions often characteristic of his day.[15] All the while he had no conviction of sin and was not truly converted. Later, Bunyan recognized that genuine conviction of sin and evangelical repentance are always present in true conversion, and he emphasizes these themes in *Pilgrim's Progress* and other writings.

Conviction of Sin and Conversion

After his pastor preached a sermon on the evil of Sabbath breaking, Bunyan began to take serious inventory of his life. He was accustomed to devoting Sundays to "delight in all manner of vice." For the first time, he felt the guilt of sin and believed that the parson had conspired to preach particularly against him. Later that day, Bunyan was convicted by God when "a voice did suddenly dart from heaven into my soul which said, Wilt thou leave thy sins and go to heaven, or have thy sins and go to hell?" He sensed the Lord looking at him with displeasure, but he thought that Christ would not forgive him. Recalling this experience, he wrote, "I felt my heart sink in despair, concluding it was too late; and therefore I resolved in my mind I would go on in sin."[16] He reasoned that since he was already damned, he might as well be damned for many sins as for a few.

Reflecting on this time, Bunyan admitted that this conclusion motivated him to "taste the sweetness" of

---

15. Bunyan, *Grace Abounding*, in *Works*, 1:7.
16. Bunyan, *Grace Abounding*, in *Works*, 1:7.

sin. He pursued sin with "as much haste" as he could, thinking that he would soon die. He later observed that many Christians face this temptation from the Devil, who seeks "to overrun their spirits with a scurvy and seared frame of heart, and benumbing of conscience." Still God continued to work in his life. Bunyan wrote of an occasion when the Lord shamed him by an ungodly woman. As he stood "cursing and swearing" near the house of "a very loose and ungodly wretch," she complained about his cursing and rebuked him, saying that he would "spoil all the youth in a whole town, if they came in [his] company."[17] Providentially, God convicted Bunyan of sin through this experience, and after the rebuke of this woman, he laid aside his cursing—even to his own amazement.

Around this same time, Bunyan began to read the Bible. Outwardly, Bunyan's life began to transform and he was convicted of some sin, but he did not know Christ. After his conversion he wrote, "Wherefore I fell to some outward reformation, both in my words and life, and did set the commandments before me for my way to heaven; which commandments I also did strive to keep, and, as I thought, did keep them pretty well sometimes, and then I should have comfort."[18] His self-righteousness increased to the point where he thought that he "pleased God as well as any man in England," and some of his neighbors began to commend him as a godly man.[19]

---

17. Bunyan, *Grace Abounding*, in *Works*, 1:9.
18. Bunyan, *Grace Abounding*, in *Works*, 1:9.
19. Bunyan, *Grace Abounding*, in *Works*, 1:10.

Bunyan took pride in the praise of men, admitting later that he "loved to be talked of as one that was truly godly." He thought that his outward behavior evidenced being a Christian, so he took consolation in the comments of others about his morality. As he later understood, he had no confidence in Christ and no assurance that he belonged to Christ. He confessed, "But poor wretch as I was, I was all this while ignorant of Jesus Christ, and going about to establish my own righteousness; and had perished therein had not God, in mercy, showed me more of my state of nature."[20]

In Bunyan's search for salvation from the condemnation of God, he traveled his own long and wrenching pilgrimage. He was a self-righteous man, numb to the truth of the gospel. Yet God showed him great mercy when he overheard a conversation between several poor Christian women discussing how miserable they were before coming to Christ. They spoke of the new birth and the work of God in their hearts—truths that Bunyan did not understand. They demonstrated remarkable joy as they talked of God's love and the abundant ways that the Lord had comforted them. Scripture laced their conversation with grace and peace, and Bunyan said it appeared "as if they had found a new world, as if they were people that dwelt alone, and were not to be reckoned among their neighbours."[21] It turned out that the women were members of the church

---

20. Bunyan, *Grace Abounding*, in *Works*, 1:10.
21. Bunyan, *Grace Abounding*, in *Works*, 1:10.

Bunyan and the Poor Women

Bunyan's meeting with the poor women, who were members of the independent church led by John Gifford, marked a turning point in his spiritual life.

pastored by John Gifford, who would eventually become Bunyan's pastor and mentor.[22]

As a result of this conversation, Bunyan began to contemplate his own lack of real spiritual life. He went back to his work but dwelled on the women's words. True conviction pinpointed his faulty foundation of good works, and a mighty upheaval occurred in his soul:

> At this I felt my own heart began to shake, as mistrusting my condition to be nought; for I saw that in all my thoughts about religion and salvation, the new birth did never enter into my mind, neither knew I the comfort of the Word and promise, nor the deceitfulness and treachery of my own wicked heart.... Thus, therefore, when I had heard and considered what they said, I left them, and went about my employment again, but their talk and discourse went with me; also my heart would tarry with them, for I was greatly affected with their words, both because by them I was convinced that I wanted the true tokens of a truly godly man, and also because by them I was convinced of the happy and blessed condition of him that was such a one.[23]

Overhearing a simple conversation among a few Christians became the means God used to arrest John Bunyan's mind from his self-dependence.

In *Pilgrim's Progress*, Bunyan gives a wonderful picture of a similar experience in the conversion of Hopeful, who lives in the town of Vanity Fair.

---

22. Calhoun, *Grace Abounding*, 17.
23. Bunyan, *Grace Abounding*, in *Works*, 1:10.

Though Christian and Faithful are manacled in a cage, Hopeful listens to their conversations and watches their lives, even in the midst of suffering. After Faithful's death, Hopeful joins himself to Christian, enters into covenant with him, and tells him that he will be his companion on the journey. Bunyan narrates, "Thus one died to make testimony to the truth, and another rises out of his ashes to be a companion with Christian in his Pilgrimage."[24]

It seems that the Holy Spirit regenerated Bunyan about this time, as evidenced by his reflection on what happened next. He found his heart especially tender to Scripture, and he was convicted by the Word of God. Unlike previous occasions when conviction resulted in superficial changes, now his whole being felt the weightiness of his sin. He testified as well to "a great bending of my mind to a continual meditating on [the gospel spoken by these poor folks], and on all other good things which at any time I heard or read of."[25] His mind, now fixed on eternity, could not be moved by the mundane issues of life. He was consumed with the kingdom of God. Bunyan had new desires for Christ and His kingdom, and he despised sin. Even though he had little knowledge, the Holy Spirit protected him from the error of those who believe that sinning liberally causes grace to abound. He admitted that their teaching would

---

24. John Bunyan, *The Pilgrim's Progress from This World to That Which Is to Come Delivered under the Similitude of a Dream*, in *Works*, 3:132.

25. Bunyan, *Grace Abounding*, in *Works*, 1:11.

have seemed very sweet to him previously, but now he saw their teaching as flawed and accursed.[26]

Bunyan was baptized by Puritan pastor John Gifford and became a member of his Separatist congregation in 1655.[27] Though Gifford's time with Bunyan was relatively brief, his influence on Bunyan's life and writings was lasting. Bunyan soaked up everything that he heard from the pulpit and read in Scripture. Reflecting on those times, Bunyan wrote, "How was my soul led from truth to truth by God!... For, to my remembrance, there was not anything that I then cried unto God to make known and reveal unto me but he was pleased to do it for me; I mean not one part of the gospel of the Lord Jesus, but I was orderly led into it." Bunyan's love for the Word of God grew and influenced all of his writings. He explained, "The Bible was precious to me in those days," as he looked into it "with new eyes." He continued, "Indeed, I was then never out of the Bible, either by reading or meditation; still crying out to God, that I might know the truth, and way to heaven and glory."[28] This characteristic of Bunyan caused C. H. Spurgeon to later comment, "Prick him anywhere; and you will find that his blood is Bibline, the very essence of the Bible flows from him. He cannot speak without quoting a text, for his soul is full of the Word of God."[29]

---

26. Bunyan, *Grace Abounding*, in *Works*, 1:11.
27. Bunyan, *Grace Abounding*, in *Works*, 1:20.
28. Bunyan, *Grace Abounding*, in *Works*, 1:11.
29. C. H. Spurgeon, *C. H. Spurgeon's Autobiography* (London: Passmore & Alabaster, 1897), 4:268.

Home of John Gifford

St. John's Rectory was the home of John Gifford, who served as minister of the Bedford independent church and whose spiritual counsel was a great help to Bunyan at the time of his conversion.

Assurance

Bunyan struggled intensely before coming to assurance in Christ. In his mind, he would vacillate between positions of salvation and damnation for weeks and months at a time, anguishing in the turmoil of no assurance for his soul. He recounted a time soon after his conversion when hardly a day passed that he did not face "a more grievous and dreadful temptation than before." The temptation, in his words, was "to sell and part with this most blessed Christ, to exchange him for the things of this life, for anything." He said that sometimes the thought, "Sell Him, sell Him, sell Him," would run endlessly through his mind. Bunyan often believed that he had consented to this temptation, and it was as though he were "tortured upon a rack for whole days together."[30] At times, he would sit down to eat a meal, and the temptation to "sell Him" would come, so he would leave the table to pray fervently. He would gain momentary relief, only to think of Esau, who sold his birthright for a bowl of porridge.

As he arose from sleep one morning, the thought occurred to him, "The blood of Christ remits all guilt." The words from the apostle John came to mind, "The blood of Jesus Christ his Son cleanseth us from all sin" (1 John 1:7). Peace filled his soul at the very thought of this triumph through Christ. This sustained him for a while, but he soon plummeted again. Each time, the Lord brought another biblical text to mind that focused on the work of Christ for the redeemed. Regular application of the

---

30. Bunyan, *Grace Abounding*, in *Works*, 1:22.

The Piety of John Bunyan

gospel became his practice. He learned to treasure the preserving power of God for His people. With that preservation, Bunyan realized that God's providence was at work even in allowing His children to endure suffering, temptation, and trials. "[God] would let David, Hezekiah, Solomon, Peter, and others fall," he wrote, "but he would not let them fall into sin unpardonable, nor into hell for sin."[31]

Bunyan was a keenly sensitive person, probably somewhat melancholy in his disposition, and this attributed to his struggles for assurance. Bunyan suffered from "a severe obsessive-compulsive disorder," according to Gaius Davies, evidenced by his repetitive struggle with the words "sell Him" and his fixation on Esau.[32] This led Bunyan to be "over-conscientious," so that he wanted "to get things absolutely *right*."[33] This inevitably promoted perfectionist tendencies. If he felt a tinge of doubt, he believed it was evidence that he did not belong to Christ. In much of Bunyan's autobiography, he gives his own testimony of inward struggles and tells how he faced those struggles with the gospel of Christ.

Davies demonstrates that Bunyan's psychological profile was not necessarily a weakness. Though he struggled for a long time, he eventually got this part of his life under control by disciplining his thoughts according to the Word of God. Davies explains that his suffering should not be called an illness; instead,

---

31. Bunyan, *Grace Abounding*, in *Works*, 1:25.

32. Gaius Davies, *Genius, Guilt, and Grace: A Doctor Looks at Suffering and Success* (Fearn, Ross-shire, Scotland: Christian Focus Publications, 2001), 65.

33. Davies, *Genius, Guilt, and Grace*, 67.

Bunyan is a good example of "how the spiritual and psychiatric aspects, though separate, are inevitably intertwined."[34] As Bunyan worked on the spiritual part of his life, it had a remarkable impact on his psychological life. Additionally, Bunyan's "over-conscientiousness had much to do with his going into and staying in prison," and that imprisonment gave us "his three greatest books."[35] The God of providence governed his life and circumstances so that the kingdom of God was enriched by his contributions, and Bunyan experienced immeasurable joy by seeking and discovering Christ during intense periods of suffering.

Bunyan found each struggle with assurance to be like a goad driving him to the Word of God. At times, Bunyan was broken and further convicted of his sinfulness by the Word, causing him to search even more desperately for the assurance he desired. In his autobiography, he explains, "Thus I went on for many weeks, sometimes comforted, and sometimes tormented, and, especially at some times my torment would be very sore, for all those Scriptures forenam'd in the *Hebrews* would be set before me, as the only sentences that would keep me out of Heaven. Then, again, I should begin to repent, that ever that thought went [through] me: I should also think thus with myself, why, How many scriptures are there against me?"[36]

---

34. Davies, *Genius, Guilt, and Grace*, 67.

35. Davies, *Genius, Guilt, and Grace*, 83. Many scholars commonly believe *Pilgrim's Progress, Grace Abounding to the Chief of Sinners,* and *Holy War* to be Bunyan's three greatest books.

36. Bunyan, *Grace Abounding*, in *Works*, 1:65–66.

The Piety of John Bunyan

But Scripture also met Bunyan in his need. On one occasion, he thought of the wickedness and blasphemy in which he had lived for so long. Because of his sensitive spirit, this drove him to the precipice, but Colossians 1:20 brought to mind that Christ has "made peace through the blood of his cross." Bunyan commented, "By which I was made to see, both again, and again, and again, that day, that God and my soul were friends by this blood; yea, I saw that the justice of God and my sinful soul could embrace and kiss each other through this blood."[37] On another occasion, he contemplated his wretchedness when Hebrews 2:14–15 came to mind: "Forasmuch then as the children are partakers of flesh and blood, he also himself likewise took part of the same; that through death he might destroy him that had the power of death, that is, the devil; and deliver them who through fear of death were all their lifetime subject to bondage." Later Bunyan wrote, "I thought that the glory of these words was then so weighty on me that I was, both once and twice, ready to swoon as I sat; yet not with grief and trouble, but with solid joy and peace."[38]

Bunyan identified the process that the Lord used to teach him. First, he was afflicted with some temptation, whether an issue involving sin or a false teaching or a trial. Then, he found refuge in Christ through the Word. He committed much Scripture to memory and regularly meditated upon it to find the

---

37. Bunyan, *Grace Abounding*, in *Works*, 1:19–20.
38. Bunyan, *Grace Abounding*, in *Works*, 1:20.

answer to his current crisis.[39] He also profited from the writing of others. A copy of Martin Luther's commentary on Galatians came into his possession, and he described the book as "so old that it was ready to fall piece from piece if I did but turn it over." Yet he devoured the book, coming to the conclusion that it spoke precisely of what he had been experiencing. He said it was "as if this book had been written out of my heart," and "I do prefer this book of Martin Luther upon the Galatians, excepting the Holy Bible, before all the books that ever I have seen, as most fit for a wounded conscience."[40]

Throughout his life, Bunyan's great consolation was Christ and His redemptive work. The more he meditated upon what Christ truly accomplished, the less he found himself retreating to the law for righteousness. Contemplating the faithfulness of Christ in the new covenant, he wrote, "Oh! I cannot now express what then I saw and felt of the steadiness of Jesus Christ, the rock of man's salvation; what was done could not be undone, added to, nor altered."[41] Thoughts of Christ's righteousness became a constant companion for Bunyan, influencing his sermons and books. Toward the end of this long, intense period of inward struggle with assurance, he was walking through a field one day when the thought struck him, "Thy righteousness is in heaven." He realized that while condemning himself for his failures, he had been trying to increase his righteous stand-

---

39. Bunyan, *Grace Abounding*, in *Works*, 1:21.
40. Bunyan, *Grace Abounding*, in *Works*, 1:22.
41. Bunyan, *Grace Abounding*, in *Works*, 1:30.

ing with God. When he did well, he felt that God was more inclined to him; when he fell into sin, he thought that his righteousness diminished. That error in thinking proved destructive to him, but he later found full assurance in the understanding that his righteousness was Christ, who was in heaven at God's right hand. Bunyan exulted in Christ and His righteousness:

> I also saw, moreover, that it was not my good frame of heart that made my righteousness better, nor yet my bad frame that made my righteousness worse; for my righteousness was Jesus Christ himself, the same yesterday, and to-day, and for ever. Heb. xiii.8....
>
> Now did my chains fall off my legs indeed, I was loosed from my affliction and irons, my temptations also fled away; so that, from that time, those dreadful scriptures of God left off to trouble me; now went I also home rejoicing, for the grace and love of God. So when I came home I looked to see if I could find that sentence, Thy righteousness is in heaven; but could not find such a saying, wherefore my heart began to sink again, only that was brought to my remembrance he "of God is made unto us wisdom, and righteousness, and sanctification, and redemption"; by this word I saw the other sentence true. 1 Co. i.30.[42]

Bunyan allegorizes this truth in *Pilgrim's Progress*, when Christian comes to the Beautiful Palace, which represents the church. Upon his arrival, he

---

42. Bunyan, *Grace Abounding*, in *Works*, 1:35–36.

Christian's Arrival at the Beautiful Palace

This illustration from an 1891 edition of *Pilgrim's Progress* depicts Christian being welcomed at the Beautiful Palace, a symbol of the visible church.

converses with three ladies—Prudence, Piety, and Charity—and they question him regarding his faith and walk in Christ. Prudence asks him about his "annoyances," referring to the areas in which he had struggled, and by what means "they were vanquished." Christian responds, "Yes, when I think what I saw at the Cross, that [the death of Christ] will do it; and when I look upon my 'broidered Coat, that [Christ's righteousness] will do it; also when I look into the Roll that I carry in my bosom, that [assurance of salvation through Christ's promises] will do it; and when my thoughts wax warm about whither I am going, that [the Celestial City] will do it."[43]

Bunyan relates through the allegory precisely what he came to embrace in his own life as he dealt with the struggles of doubt and depression. He looked to Christ's death on his behalf, Christ's righteousness imputed to him, the assuring promises in the gospel, and the anticipation of being with Christ in heaven.

Church Membership and Preaching Ministry

Joining a Baptist church in Bunyan's day was an extended process that involved the entire congregation. The minister examined the person for sincere repentance and belief in the gospel, and several church members would assess the person's moral character. Once they were satisfied of the inquirer's seriousness, he attended a private church meeting in which the members decided whether or not to receive him into their fellowship. If received, he

---

43. Bunyan, *Pilgrim's Progress*, in *Works*, 3:108.

would be baptized, if needed, and then admitted to the Lord's Table.[44]

Shortly upon Bunyan's admittance to the Lord's Table, he faced new temptations and spiritual unrest. This period of struggle lasted for nine months, and once again the Lord met him in the Scripture and brought comfort to his troubled soul. During this time, Bunyan believed he was "somewhat inclining to a consumption," or tuberculosis. Physically weak, he fell into another slump in his spirit. Though recalling God's goodness to him in preceding days, he also began to dredge up sins from the past. Bunyan wrote, "At the apprehension of these things my sickness was doubled upon me, for now was I sick in my inward man, my soul was clogged with guilt; now also was my former experience of God's goodness to me quite taken out of my mind, and hid as if it had never been, nor seen."[45] Though dismayed, Bunyan found comfort in the Word by the Holy Spirit:

> Now was my soul greatly pinched between these two considerations, Live I must not, Die I dare not; now I sunk and fell in my spirit, and was giving up all for lost; but as I was walking up and down in the house, as a man in a most woful [*sic*] state, that word of God took hold of my heart, Ye are "justified freely by his grace, through the redemption that is in Christ Jesus." Ro. iii.24. But oh what a turn it made upon me!
>
> [It was as if God said]… "Sinner, thou thinkest that because of thy sins and infirmities I

---

44. Bunyan, *Grace Abounding*, in *Works*, 1:39, editor's note.
45. Bunyan, *Grace Abounding*, in *Works*, 1:39.

cannot save thy soul, but behold my Son is by me, and upon him I look, and not on thee, and will deal with thee according as I am pleased with him." At this I was greatly lightened in my mind, and made to understand that God could justify a sinner at any time; it was but his looking upon Christ, and imputing of his benefits to us, and the work was forthwith done.[46]

As Bunyan grew in faith, he continued to understand the definitive work of the Holy Spirit in believers. The Spirit brought conviction of sin over and over again to his soul. The Holy Spirit also illuminated Scripture and helped him through various trials and tribulations. Harry Poe explains:

Bunyan further understood these words as having been brought to him by the Spirit. The periods of distress lasted for moments, weeks, and even years before Bunyan found peace for what troubled him. Because of the power of the Word to give him comfort and hope in his lengthy conversion experience, the objective word of Scripture continued to play a primary role in the form Bunyan's theology would take.[47]

After he had been five or six years in the faith, the church recognized Bunyan's gifts for ministering the Word. As customary with nonconformist churches, the congregation asked him to offer a word of exhortation in private meetings. He wrote that he did so "in private, though with much weakness and

---

46. Bunyan, *Grace Abounding*, in *Works*, 1:39.
47. Harry Poe, "John Bunyan," in *Baptist Theologians*, ed. Timothy George and David Dockery (Nashville: Broadman, 1990), 32–33.

infirmity" as he began to perceive his gifts for ministry.[48] The church again acknowledged the blessing of Bunyan's ministry to them, and they invited him to assist in gospel ministry among the poor in other villages. God continued to bless Bunyan, and the church pressed him to engage in the preaching ministry. He prayed and fasted over the decision and concluded that God had called him to ministry, even though he still struggled with "the fiery darts of the Devil concerning [his] eternal state."[49]

Though "with great fear and trembling at the sight of [his] own weakness," Bunyan sought to preach the Word according to the gifts and abilities entrusted to him. His lively preaching had an immediate impact on the region, with people coming great distances to hear him proclaim the gospel. By his own record, once people in the area found out about him, "they came in to hear the Word by hundreds, and that from all parts, though upon sundry and divers accounts.... I had not preached long before some began to be touched by the Word, and to be greatly afflicted in their minds at the apprehension of the greatness of their sin, and of their need of Jesus Christ."[50] Bunyan was stunned that people wanted to listen to his preaching of the gospel, and even more stunned by the testimonies of those affected by his messages.

His preaching came with such passion, power, and clarity that even the greatest theologian of the

---

48. Bunyan, *Grace Abounding*, in *Works*, 1:41.
49. Bunyan, *Grace Abounding*, in *Works*, 1:40–41.
50. Bunyan, *Grace Abounding*, in *Works*, 1:41.

Bunyan Preaching

Bunyan had an itinerant ministry and often preached in the open air to accommodate the large crowds that flocked to hear him.

day, John Owen, "told King Charles II that he would gladly trade all his learning for Bunyan's power to preach."[51] At first, Bunyan's gospel preaching focused on God's law and the condemnation of all flesh due to original sin. Bunyan wrote, "Now this part of my work I fulfilled with great sense; for the terrors of the law, and guilt for my transgressions, lay heavy on my conscience. I preached what I felt, what I smartingly did feel, even that under which my poor soul did groan and tremble to astonishment."[52] Because he felt such a deep consciousness of his own sinfulness, he communicated the same biblical reality to his audiences. Often, Bunyan felt such keenness of his own sinfulness that terror seized him as he entered the pulpit, only to know liberty from the Lord as he began to preach.

For two years, his preaching continually focused on the theme of man's sinfulness. But after that time, he became so affected by "many sweet discoveries of [Christ's] blessed grace" that he altered his preaching. He labored "to hold forth Jesus Christ in all his offices, relations, and benefits unto the world; and did strive also to discover, to condemn, and remove those false supports and props on which the world doth both lean, and by them fall and perish." As the evolution of his preaching continued, he emphasized "the mystery of union with Christ." He identified "three chief points of the Word of God," which he maintained for five years, namely, man's sinfulness;

---

51. J. I. Packer, "*Pilgrim's Progress* by John Bunyan (1628–1688)," in *The Devoted Life: An Invitation to the Puritan Classics*, ed. Kelly Kapic and Randall Gleason (Downers Grove, Ill.: InterVarsity, 2004), 184.

52. Bunyan, *Grace Abounding*, in *Works*, 1:42.

John Owen (1616–1683)

John Owen was a distinguished Puritan theologian, Oxford scholar, and one of the greatest Reformed theologians.

Christ in His offices as prophet, priest, and king; and the mystery of union with Christ.[53]

Bunyan's utter dependence on God was evident in his preaching ministry. He would wait for God to burden him with a particular place to preach, which he described as "the going of God upon my spirit to desire I might preach there." He observed that whenever it seemed that God would do a saving work among a people, "there the Devil hath begun to roar in the hearts, and by the mouths of his servants." He explained, "Yea, oftentimes when the wicked world that raged most, there hath been souls awaked by the Word." Bunyan, like the apostle Paul, longed to preach the gospel to people who had never heard of God's grace. He wrote,

> My great desire in my fulfilling my ministry was to get into the darkest places of the country, even amongst those people that were furthest off of profession; yet not because I could not endure the light, for I feared not to show my gospel to any, but because I found my spirit leaned most after awakening and converting work, and the Word that I carried did lead itself most that way also; "Yea, so have I strived to preach the gospel, not where Christ was named, lest I should build upon another man's foundation." Ro. xv.20.[54]

Bunyan cared not for applause or commendation. He desired genuine, Spirit-wrought conversions to Christ evidenced by "a heart set on fire to be saved by Christ, with strong breathing after a truly sanctified

---

53. Bunyan, *Grace Abounding*, in *Works*, 1:42.
54. Bunyan, *Grace Abounding*, in *Works*, 1:43.

soul; that it was that delighted me; those were the souls I counted blessed." However, Bunyan constantly encountered obstacles on his own pilgrimage in preaching the gospel. The severe temptation to blaspheme Christ returned, often pressing him with such obstinacy that he feared he would mouth his blasphemies from the pulpit. The Adversary came against him as well, trying to intimidate him to stop preaching truth. He felt the Devil saying to him, "What, will you preach this? This condemns yourself; of this your own soul is guilty; wherefore preach not of it at all." But God enabled him to have the same spirit that gave Samson strength to bow with all of his might in Dagon's temple, crying, "Let me die with the Philistines" (Judg. 16:29–30). Bunyan wrote, "It is far better that thou do judge thyself, even by preaching plainly to others, than that thou, to save thyself, imprison the truth in unrighteousness; blessed be God for his help also in this."[55]

The sin of pride tormented him often during his preaching. However, his sin forced him to rely on Christ, and he counted it joyous to see this, commenting, "For it hath been my every day's portion to be let into the evil of my own heart, and still made to see such a multitude of corruptions and infirmities therein, that it hath caused hanging down of the head under all my gifts and attainments; I have felt this thorn in the flesh, the very mercy of God to me. 2 Co. xii.7–9."[56] Bunyan saw pride as a mirror into his own soul, reminding him of his own weakness

---
55. Bunyan, *Grace Abounding*, in *Works*, 1:44.
56. Bunyan, *Grace Abounding*, in *Works*, 1:44.

in spite of commendations for his preaching. He learned not to listen to men's praise but to understand that he preached only by God's great mercy. Bunyan believed that the preacher

> hath also cause to walk humbly with God, and be little in his own eyes, and to remember withal, that his gifts are not his own, but the church's; and that by them he is made a servant to the church; and he must give at last an account of his stewardship unto the Lord Jesus; and to give a good account, will be a blessed thing.... Let all men therefore prize a little with the fear of the Lord; gifts indeed are desirable, but yet great grace and small gifts are better than great gifts and no grace.[57]

Arrest and Imprisonment

After Bunyan had preached for about five years, he went to a group of "good people in the country" in order to preach the gospel.[58] During this time, Bunyan crossed the legal line drawn by Charles II by holding illegal "conventicles" for the preaching of the gospel. He was arrested and thrown into the Bedford jail to await a hearing from a local justice. Bunyan offered security that he would not flee before his initial hearing, but the authorities did not accept his bond, evidently because he would not cease to preach the gospel if released. As a man of conviction, Bunyan would not quit preaching the gospel because of man's foolish laws.

---

57. Bunyan, *Grace Abounding*, in *Works*, 1:45.
58. Bunyan, *Grace Abounding*, in *Works*, 1:47.

Prison on Bedford Bridge

An illustration of the town jail, which was a part of the main bridge over the River Great Ouse. A plaque on the present bridge states that Bunyan served his second imprisonment of 1676 here.

In Bunyan's own words, "I was indicted for an upholder and maintainer of unlawful assemblies and conventicles, and for not conforming to the national worship of the Church of England." He was quite honest with the justices, telling them that he intended to continue preaching the gospel. Consequently, they sentenced him to "perpetual banishment, because [he] refused to conform."[59] From November 1660 until his release in late 1672, Bunyan spent twelve years in the Bedford jail for preaching the gospel.[60] He could have been released at any time if he promised never to preach unlawfully again, but the burden of the gospel and the calling of God would not allow Bunyan to relent for the comforts of freedom. He saw his time in jail as a blessing from God, and some of his greatest works were penned during imprisonment. He explained:

> I never had in all my life so great an inlet into the Word of God as now [that is, while in prison]; those Scriptures that I saw nothing in before, are made in this place and state to shine upon me; Jesus Christ also was never more real and apparent than now; here I have seen him and felt him indeed: O that word, We have not preached unto you cunningly devised fables (2 Pe. i.16); and that, God raised Christ from the dead, and gave him glory, that your faith and hope might be in God (1 Pe. i.2), were blessed words unto me in this my imprisoned condition....

---

59. Bunyan, *Grace Abounding*, in *Works*, 1:47.
60. Bunyan, *Grace Abounding*, in *Works*, 1:47, editor's note.

> I have had sweet sights of the forgiveness of my sins in this place, and of my being with Jesus in another world.... I never knew what it was for God to stand by me at all turns, and at every offer of Satan "to afflict me," as I have found him since I came in hither; for look how fears have presented themselves, so have supports and encouragements, yea, when I have started, even as it were at nothing else but my shadow, yet God, as being very tender of me, hath not suffered me to be molested, but would with one scripture and another strengthen me against all; insomuch that I have often said, Were it lawful, I could pray for greater trouble, for the greater comfort's sake (Ec. vii.14, 2 Co. i.5).[61]

Prior to his arrest, Bunyan knew that continued preaching of the gospel might lead to his imprisonment. Yet he willingly risked his freedom to preach the gospel to those in need. For a year before his arrest, he had two thoughts that regularly came to mind. First, he wondered if he could endure imprisonment, especially an extended sentence. He found joy in the prayer of the apostle Paul, that he might be "strengthened with all might, according to his glorious power, unto all patience and long-suffering with joyfulness" (Col. 1:11). He would not grimly resign to his fate; he wanted to endure as a joyful Christian. Second, he thought of how he might face death if God were pleased to take him. The possibility of death brought to mind Paul's statement to the Corinthians, "But we had the sentence of death in

---

61. Bunyan, *Grace Abounding*, in *Works*, 1:47.

ourselves, that we should not trust in ourselves, but in God which raiseth the dead" (2 Cor. 1:9). Bunyan wrote: "By this scripture I was made to see, that if ever I would suffer rightly, I must first pass a sentence of death upon everything that can properly be called a thing of this life, even to reckon myself, my wife, my children, my health, my enjoyments, and all, as dead to me, and myself as dead to them."[62]

In Bunyan's own words, he knew that he must "live upon God that is invisible."[63] John Piper points to this as the key statement that explains Bunyan's remarkable Christian life and ministry.[64] Bunyan found the same comfort that the apostle Paul alludes to in his letter to the Corinthians: "While we look not at the things which are seen, but at the things which are not seen: for the things which are seen are temporal; but the things which are not seen are eternal" (2 Cor. 4:18).

Bunyan did not want to brace himself for one level of suffering only to face a more intense level. He believed if he prayerfully prepared only for imprisonment, but not for the whip, then he might be overcome by a flogging. He concluded, "I see the best way to go through sufferings is to trust in God through Christ, as touching the world to come; and as touching this world, to count 'the grave my house, to make my bed in darkness, and to say to corruption, Thou art my father, and to the worm, Thou art my mother and my sister.' That is,

---

62. Bunyan, *Grace Abounding*, in *Works*, 1:48.
63. Bunyan, *Grace Abounding*, in *Works*, 1:48.
64. John Piper, *The Hidden Smile of God* (Wheaton, Ill.: Crossway, 2001), 43.

to familiarize these things to me."[65] He likely found consolation from reading Foxe's *Book of Martyrs,* as well as stories of other Puritans who suffered for the gospel during the cruel reign of Archbishop Laud (1633–1641).[66]

Bunyan's suffering was exacerbated by the anguish of separation from his family. Bunyan's first wife died in 1658, leaving him with four children under the age of ten. The following year, he married an eighteen-year-old named Elizabeth who proved to be an excellent helper to him, as well as a vocal defender before the authorities. Bunyan deeply loved his oldest child, Mary, who was born blind and whom he refers to in his autobiography as "my poor blind child, who lay nearer my heart than all I had besides." They lived on a meager wage, so Bunyan's incarceration meant that his family faced begging to survive. He described this knowledge "as the pulling the flesh from my bones," yet he said to his family, "I must venture you all with God, though it goeth to the quick to leave you." His reasoning was founded on a good and sovereign God: "I had also this consideration, that if I should now venture all for God, I engaged God to take care of my concernments; but if I forsook him and his ways, for fear of any trouble that should come to me or mine, then I should not only falsify my profession, but should count also that my concernments were not so sure, if left at

---

65. Bunyan, *Grace Abounding,* in *Works,* 1:48.
66. Calhoun, *Grace Abounding,* 26; Bunyan, *Grace Abounding,* in *Works,* 1:48, editor's note.

Bunyan in Prison

An illustration depicts the imprisoned Bunyan parting from his blind daughter, Mary.

God's feet, while I stood to and for his name, as they would be, if they were under my own [care]."[67]

Bunyan constantly encountered despair and despondency, especially when first imprisoned. He felt himself sinking deeper and deeper, and his writings reveal his despair: "I was not fit to die, neither indeed did think I could, if I should be called to it." As he labored through these dark days, light finally came. Bunyan explained, "Thus was I tossed for many weeks, and knew not what to do.... At last this consideration fell with weight upon me, That it was for the Word and way of God, that I was in this condition, wherefore I was engaged not to flinch a hair's breadth from it."[68] Even so, his desire to fulfill God's will was often overtaken by a temptation to deny God. The most severe temptations he faced questioned the being of God and the truth of His gospel. At such times, he thought God would pour out severe chastisement upon him; instead, he found them as times for "the discovery of his grace."[69]

Bunyan's writings offer a candid look at his struggles, and he identifies "seven abominations," as he calls them, that afflicted his heart. These seven abominations included:

> (1) inclinings to unbelief; (2) suddenly to forget the love and mercy that Christ manifesteth; (3) a leaning to the works of the law; (4) wanderings and coldness in prayer; (5) to forget to watch for [the things] that I pray for; (6) apt to murmur

---

67. Bunyan, *Grace Abounding*, in *Works*, 1:48.
68. Bunyan, *Grace Abounding*, in *Works*, 1:49.
69. Bunyan, *Grace Abounding*, in *Works*, 1:49–50.

because I have no more, and yet ready to abuse what I have; (7) I can do none of those things which God commands me, but my corruptions will thrust in themselves, "When I would do good, evil is present with me."[70]

Bunyan's obsessive-compulsive, perfectionist tendencies caused him to struggle with unbelief and lean toward the works of the law. Aspects of his life that others would never notice often glared in his mind. Bunyan learned that even with the tendencies toward these abominations, God was at work to instruct him and bring him more into the radiant experience of Christ.

Mirroring his seven abominations, Bunyan perceived seven ways that the Lord ordered his abominations for his good: "(1) They make me abhor myself; (2) they keep me from trusting my heart; (3) they convince me of the insufficiency of all inherent righteousness; (4) they show me the necessity of flying to Jesus; (5) they press me to pray unto God; (6) they show me the need I have to watch and be sober; and (7) they provoke me to look to God, through Christ, to help me, and carry me through this world. Amen."[71]

These seven areas of divine blessing demonstrate Bunyan's own insufficiency in living unto Christ. He daily needed to rest in Christ, venturing all upon God. Christ was everything for him as a believer.

---

70. Bunyan, *Grace Abounding*, in *Works*, 1:49–50.
71. Bunyan, *Grace Abounding*, in *Works*, 1:49–50.

Pilgrim's Progress

As an author, Bunyan composed poetry, allegories in novel fashion, children's books, theological works, and expositions of Scripture. One Bunyan scholar lists fifty-eight books that he wrote.[72] During his second imprisonment, Bunyan likely completed his most famous book, *Pilgrim's Progress*.[73] His time in prison shaped his faith and piety, and those twelve years had an extraordinary influence on his writings. A century later, George Whitefield said of *Pilgrim's Progress*, "It smells of the prison. It was written when the author was confined in Bedford jail. And ministers never write or preach so well as when under the cross: the Spirit of Christ and of Glory then rests upon them."[74] John Owen's publisher, urged by Owen, ran the first edition of *Pilgrim's Progress* in 1678.[75] The book ran through three editions in the first year, and the tinker-turned-preacher became a household name in England.

Pilgrim's Progress details Christian's conversion and the following spiritual journey, focusing on the themes of sanctification and perseverance in the lives of believers. Jeff Robinson calls these "the twin foci of all of ministry" with the Puritans: "For in Puritan thought conversion was always related

---

72. Christopher Hill, *A Tinker and a Poor Man: John Bunyan and His Church, 1628–1688* (New York: Alfred A. Knopf, 1989), xv–xvii.

73. Calhoun, *Grace Abounding*, 34–35.

74. Barry Horner, The Pilgrim's Progress: *An Evangelical Apologetic, Themes and Issues* (Lindenhurst, N.Y.: Reformation Press Publishing, 1998), iii.

75. Packer, *"Pilgrim's Progress,"* 184.

THE
Pilgrim's Progreſs
FROM
THIS WORLD,
TO
That which is to come:

Delivered under the Similitude of a

DREAM

Wherein is Diſcovered,
The manner of his ſetting out,
His Dangerous Journey; And ſafe
Arrival at the Deſired Countrey.

I have uſed Similitudes, Hoſ. 12. 10.

By *John Bunyan*.

Licenſed and Entred according to Order.

LONDON,
Printed for *Nath. Ponder* at the *Peacock*
in the *Poultrey* near *Cornhil*, 1678.

Title Page from the First Edition of *Pilgrim's Progress*

The Piety of John Bunyan

to the entire Christian life."[76] The influence of *Pilgrim's Progress* on later generations of Christians and pastors cannot be overstated. The great nineteenth-century English preacher C. H. Spurgeon made it a practice to read *Pilgrim's Progress* each year to glean the same passion for biblical ministry that captured Bunyan. Today, the book is a classic work "translated into more than 200 languages and to date is the second best-selling book in the history of the English language after the Bible."[77] Bunyan scholar Roger Sharrock points out that among "English readers it is bound to appear as the supreme classic of the English Puritan tradition."[78]

Why did the book make such an impact in Bunyan's day and in the more than three hundred years since? J. I. Packer explains that "it stands as a full-scale index in picture form to the entire range of the Puritan understanding of Christian existence. The themes and images in both parts are biblical, and all the ups and downs of real and phony Christianity are presented for the reader's instruction and self-assessment."[79] Bunyan's method in the book is threefold:

> First, to picture personal spiritual life as a pilgrimage—a trek to a religiously significant destination, in this case heaven, the Celestial City. Second, to develop Jesus' image of the pilgrim path as straight, narrow and taxing, by dotting

---

76. Robinson, 4.

77. Robinson, 1.

78. Roger Sharrock, introduction to *The Pilgrim's Progress*, by John Bunyan, ed. Roger Sharrock (Harmondsworth, U.K.: Penguin, 1965), 7.

79. Packer, *"Pilgrim's Progress,"* 184.

it with dangers and false trails alongside its helps and helpers. Third, to follow real-life individuals bearing character-label names through the ups and downs of their travels along it, seeing sights, visiting places, overcoming obstacles, resolving problems, and relating to friends, foes, fools and failures whom they meet en route.[80]

Packer points out five key themes that dominate *Pilgrim's Progress* and reverberate throughout much of Bunyan's writings. First, "the good word" highlights the Reformation and Puritan emphasis on the centrality of Scripture to every detail of life and eternity. Second, "the good news" maintains the common theme of "the gospel as the Reformers had proclaimed it." Third, "the good way" represents the journey of Christian sanctification and perseverance, which is the overarching theme of the book. Fourth, "the good guide" emphasizes the need for effective pastoral work in the body of Christ. Fifth, "the good end" models dying in Puritan thought.[81]

Perhaps better than any other work, *Pilgrim's Progress* encapsulates the idea of Christians as sojourners who face hardships and suffering in a strange and dangerous world. Throughout the allegorical journey, Christian encounters dangers, pitfalls, and snares on his way to heaven, but it is the progressive and civilized town of Vanity Fair where the greatest persecution takes place. Though they do nothing to provoke the citizens of Vanity Fair, the pilgrims greatly offend the townspeople with their clothing,

---

80. Packer, *"Pilgrim's Progress,"* 185.
81. Packer, *"Pilgrim's Progress,"* 188–98.

speech, and lifestyle. The townspeople therefore "took them and beat them, and besmeared them with dirt, and then put them into the Cage, that they might be made a Spectacle to all the men of the Fair."[82]

Next, Christian and Faithful face a mock trial and condemnation by the city. The townspeople return a guilty verdict and call for a cruel death. Bunyan describes Faithful's punishment: "They therefore brought him out, to do with him according to their Law; and first they scourged him, then they buffeted him, then they lanced his flesh with knives: after that they stoned him with stones, then pricked him with their swords; and last of all, they burnt him to ashes at the Stake. Thus came Faithful to his end."[83]

Meanwhile, Christian escapes by "he that overrules all things, having the Power of their rage in his own Hand," and continues on his journey.[84] Thus Bunyan, writing from prison and acutely aware of the persecution during his day, vividly captures the experience of many believers throughout history, especially in the sixteenth and seventeenth centuries.

Other Writings from Prison

Prison tends to bring out the worst and best in men. In Bunyan's case, prison had an important role in the formation of his personal piety, as revealed in his prison writings. Rather than causing him to seethe in bitterness, Bunyan's bonds gave him cause for thanksgiving. Suffering often breeds a spirit

---

82. Bunyan, *Pilgrim's Progress*, in *Works*, 128.
83. Bunyan, *Pilgrim's Progress*, in *Works*, 131–32.
84. Bunyan, *Pilgrim's Progress*, in *Works*, 132.

of resentment and rancor, but Bunyan's joy was founded on God's truth. He wrote, "The sufferings of the saints are of a redeeming virtue.... By their patient enduring and losing their blood for the word they recover the truths of God that have been burned in Antichristian rubbish, from that soil and slur that thereby hath for a long time cleaved unto them."[85]

Bunyan penned his "Prison Meditations Directed to the Heart of Suffering Saints and Reigning Sinners" in 1665 while still in prison.[86] These seventy stanzas reveal the practice of piety in Bunyan's own walk and offer encouragement to any Christian walking through suffering. Growth in grace marked the days of his imprisonment, and he recovered many truths that he would not have recognized apart from the loneliness and solitude provided by his prison cell. The days of suffering were not wasted on complaining and grumbling because Bunyan knew the presence of Christ and contemplated His Word. He wrote,

> I am, indeed, in prison now
> In body, but my mind
> Is free to study Christ, and how
> Unto me he is kind.[87]

His persecutors might lock him behind bars, but they could not bar him from Christ:

---

85. John Bunyan, "Paul's Departure and Crown," in *Works*, 1:724.

86. John Bunyan, "Prison Meditations Directed to the Heart of Suffering Saints and Reigning Sinners," in *The Works of John Bunyan*, ed. George Offor (1854; repr., Edinburgh: Banner of Truth, 1991), 1:*63–*66.

87. Bunyan, "Prison Meditations," in *Works*, 1:*64 (stanza 5).

> For though men keep my outward man
>   Within their locks and bars,
> Yet by faith of Christ I can
>   Mount higher than the stars.
>
> Their fetters cannot spirits tame,
>   Nor tie up God from me;
> My faith and hope they cannot lame,
>   Above them I shall be.[88]

Rather than stifle his life, he said of the confines of prison, "I here am very much refreshed."[89] Who could make such a statement apart from intense devotion to Jesus Christ? His time in jail not wasted, Bunyan "refreshed" himself in the Lord through the Word of God and prayer. Bunyan described prayer as "a sincere, sensible, affectionate pouring out of the heart or soul to God, through Christ, in the strength and assistance of the Holy Spirit, for such things as God hath promised, or according to the Word, for the good of the church, with submission, in faith, to the will of God."[90] His pastoral exhortation came out of experience. For Bunyan, prayer's ultimate aim was the relationship it engendered with God. He wrote, "There is in prayer an unbosoming of a man's self, an opening of the heart to God, an affectionate pouring out of the soul in requests, sighs, and

---

88. Bunyan, "Prison Meditations," in *Works*, 1:*64 (stanzas 6–7).

89. Bunyan, "Prison Meditations," in *Works*, 1:*64 (stanza 8).

90. John Bunyan, "I Will Pray with the Spirit and with the Understanding Also, or A Discourse Touching Prayer Wherein Is Briefly Discovered, 1. What Prayer Is. 2. What It Is to Pray with the Spirit. 3. What It Is to Pray with the Spirit and with the Understanding Also," in *Works*, 1:623.

groans.... Right prayer sees nothing substantial, and worth the looking after, but God."[91]

Contentment lay at the foundation of Bunyan's peace in prison. His regular practice of meditation upon Scripture, clinging to the promises of God, and finding deep satisfaction in the gospel helped to maintain a contented spirit. His persecutors thought they could silence his preaching and break his spirit, but contentment with Christ trumped their efforts. Bunyan wrote,

> If they do give me gall to drink,
>   Then God doth sweet'ning cast
> So much thereto, that they can't think
>   How bravely it doth taste.

The Devil might set "heaviness and grief" before him, yet, "so God sets Christ and grace much more, / Whereby I take relief."[92]

Contemplation of another world often strengthened Bunyan while he waited for release so that he might rejoin his family and church. He looked heavenward and patiently awaited the promised inheritance in Christ. Because of this promise, Bunyan exuded joy from the Bedford jail. The tone of his poetry from prison evidences complete satisfaction in Christ with a view to eternal inheritance:

> This [jail] to us is as a hill,
>   From whence we plainly see

---

91. Bunyan, *Grace Abounding*, in *Works*, 1:7. Bunyan cites Psalms 38:9; 42:2, 4; 62:8; 71:1–5; Deuteronomy 4:29; and 1 Timothy 5:5 to demonstrate the biblical emphasis on "unbosoming" the heart in prayer.

92. Bunyan, "Prison Meditations," in *Works*, 1:*64 (stanzas 22–23).

Beyond this world, and take our fill
    Of things that lasting be.

From hence we see the emptiness
    Of all this world contains;
And here we feel the blessedness
    That for us yet remains....

When he our righteousness forth brings
    Bright shining as the day,
And wipeth off those sland'rous things
    That scorners on us lay.

We see our earthly happiness
    For heavenly house and home;
We leave this world because 'tis less,
    And worse than that to come....

Again, we see what glory 'tis
    Freely to bear our cross
For him, who for us took up his,
    When he our servant was.[93]

Critics castigated Bunyan for neglecting family and liberties by his intransigence toward the government, but he remained steadfast to his convictions regarding gospel preaching and Scripture. Seeking not the approval of man, he explained his position: "The judgment that is made of our sufferings by carnal men is nothing at all to be heeded; they see not the glory that is wrapped up in our cause, nor the innocence and goodness of our conscience in our enduring of these afflictions; they judge according to the flesh, according to outward appearance."

---

93. Bunyan, "Prison Meditations," in *Works*, 1:*65 (stanzas 34–35, 43–44, 48).

He found satisfaction that, in spite of the contempt shown toward him, "all things are here converted to another use and end."[94] For Bunyan, devotion to Christ was much more valuable and rewarding than earthly comfort and possessions. He wrote,

> Who now dare say we throw away
>   our goods or liberty,
> When God's most holy Word doth say
>   We gain thus much thereby?[95]

Endless hours of poring over Scripture, absorbing it as his very food, filled Bunyan's consciousness with an understanding of the ways of God with His servants.

Conclusion

Bunyan was officially released in 1672 when Charles II issued the Declaration of Indulgence giving "religious freedom 'to all his loving subjects,' including Roman Catholics and nonconformists."[96] During Bunyan's imprisonment, the jailer allowed him to return home and preach in the Bedford Baptist church on several occasions, and upon his release, he served as pastor of the Bedford church. Less than five years later, the Anglican bishops urged the king to suppress the meetings of Dissenters, and Bunyan's license to preach was revoked for not taking Communion in the state church. Bunyan was sent back to the Bedford jail late in 1676. In his own words, he was "had home to prison again," spending six months in

---

94. Bunyan, "Paul's Departure and Crown," in *Works*, 1:725.
95. Bunyan, "Prison Meditations," in *Works*, 1:*65 (stanza 52).
96. Nichols, *Pages from Church History*, 209.

Bunyan Old Meeting

Top: The Bunyan Old Meeting, built in 1707, replaced the barn where the church met when Bunyan was pastor. *Bottom*: The present Bunyan Meeting was built in 1849 and houses the Bunyan Museum.

jail before his release in June 1677.[97] Bunyan spent one-fifth of his life in the Bedford jail. Yet, by God's grace, he made it profitable and fruitful for the kingdom of God. Rather than sulking and complaining, he used his time for study, meditation, writing, and ministry. He regularly preached to those in jail, and on one occasion he preached to a whole congregation that had been arrested.

Bunyan accepted the call as pastor of the Baptist church in Bedford during his first prison sentence and remained there until his death. According to estimates, there were about 120 nonconformist parishioners in Bedford when he began serving as pastor. Though many urged him to move to London for a bigger church, Bunyan stayed with the Bedford congregation, shepherding them faithfully. He sometimes traveled to London and other cities to preach, and "in the days of toleration, a day's notice would get a crowd of 1,200 to hear him preach at 7 o'clock in the morning on a weekday."[98]

Like the pastoral characters in *Pilgrim's Progress*, he regularly engaged his congregation and others in pastoral ministry. The application portions of his sermons were saturated with pointed pastoral care. Piper points out, "Bunyan's writings were an extension of his pastoral ministry, mainly to his flock in Bedford, who lived in constant danger of harassment and prison. His suffering fit him well for the task."[99] As part of his pastoral ministry, he often was

---

97. Bunyan, *Grace Abounding*, in *Works*, 1:47.
98. Piper, *Hidden Smile of God*, 53.
99. Piper, *Hidden Smile of God*, 62.

called upon to help reconcile broken relationships, and in August 1688, he traveled to London to mend a broken relationship between a father and son. He contracted a fever on the way back and died of either pneumonia or the flu.[100] Following his death on August 31, 1688, Bunyan was buried two days later in Bunhill Fields, the nonconformist cemetery. Today, Bunyan's tomb stands on a concrete walkway with his likeness, as well as figures from *Pilgrim's Progress,* carved from stone as a memorial to his lasting influence on Christ's people.

Throughout his life, a broken, contrite heart and a spirit of true repentance forced Bunyan to rely solely on God's mercy. Piety is often born from adversity as suffering saints throw themselves on the grace of God. From imprisonment to struggles with assurance and pride, Bunyan's life was an incubator for nurturing a pious life completely devoted to God and the gospel. At every turn, Bunyan looked to God and the gospel to steer his life, even in the face of ridicule and bodily harm. In many ways,

---

100. Editor George Offor adds an introductory note to Bunyan's last sermon regarding the events surrounding his death: "The disease which terminated his invaluable life, was brought on by a journey to Reading on horseback, undertaken with the benevolent design of reconciling an offended father to his son. Having accomplished his object, he rode to London; on his way home, through a heavy rain, the effects of which appeared soon after this.... He bore, with most exemplary patience and resignation, the fever which invaded his body; and, at a distance from his wife and family, in the house of his friend Mr. Strudwick, at Snow Hill, his pilgrimage was ended, and he fell asleep in perfect peace, to awake amidst the harmonies and glory of the celestial city" (George Offor, Advertisement by the Editor, in "Mr. Bunyan's Last Sermon, Preached August 19, 1688," in *Works*, 2:755).

Bunyan's imprisonment was his own choice—he could have refrained from preaching the gospel and been released at any time. But as a slave to Christ, he could not submit to the demands of the English government.

As he stood before Justice Keelin, who threatened Bunyan with banishment from the realm if he insisted on preaching the gospel, Bunyan replied, "If I was out of prison to-day I would preach the gospel again to-morrow, by the help of God."[101] Despite years behind bars, Bunyan never wavered. The gospel was too precious for him to be silent in order to be free of jail. "Come, be of good cheer," he wrote while imprisoned. "Let us not be daunted; our cause is good, we need not be ashamed of it; to preach God's Word is so good a work, that we shall be well rewarded, if we suffer for that."[102]

Bunyan ventured all for God even when faced with prison, persecution, deprivation, and loss. He understood the "holy war" in which the Christian constantly lives, that apart from consciously living in Christ and the gospel, he would not survive. His devotion to Christ, whether in prison or shepherding his flock, kept him anchored as a faithful Christian. His piety was no accident but rather a display of venturing all upon God.

---

101. Bunyan, *Grace Abounding*, in *Works*, 1:56–57.
102. Bunyan, *Grace Abounding*, in *Works*, 1:51.

Bunyan's Tomb

Bunyan is buried at Bunhill Fields, London, which was a burial ground for dissenters.

(photo courtesy of Kbthompson at en.wikipedia)

SECTION ONE

Christ Our Advocate

St. John's Church

The independent congregation of Bedford, led by John Gifford, met in this building when Bunyan joined the church.

1

Advantages and Privileges for Those Who Have Jesus Christ as Advocate

An...advantage that those who have Jesus Christ as their advocate is this: He is always ready, always in court, always with the Judge then and there to oppose if our accuser comes, pleading against him what is pleadable for His children. And the text implies this where it says, "We have an advocate with the Father" [1 John 2:1], always with the Father. Some lawyers, though they are otherwise able and shrewd, yet not being always in court and ready, do suffer their poor clients to be baffled and nonsuited[1] by their adversary. Because of this neglect, a judgment is made against the client for whom the advocate has undertaken to plead, to the client's great perplexity and damage. But Satan can have no such opportunity with our Advocate, for He is with the Father—always with the Father—as to be a Priest, so to be an Advocate: "We have an advocate with the Father," always with the Father.

From *The Work of Jesus Christ as an Advocate*: *Clearly Explained, and Largely Improved, for the Benefit of All Believers*, in *Works*, 1:180–82.

1. *nonsuit*: A judge stops the suit when, in his opinion, a plaintiff fails to prosecute a case or brings insufficient evidence.

Also, the book of Hebrews shows us the carefulness of our Advocate, where it says He is gone "into heaven itself, now to appear in the presence of God for us" (Heb. 9:24). *Now*, just the time present; *now*, the time always present; *now*, let Satan come when he will! Nor is it to be omitted that this word *now* that thus specifies the time, the present time, does also conclude it to be that time in which we are imperfect in grace, in which we have many failings, in which we are tempted and accused of the Devil to God; this is the time, and in it, and every moment of it, He now appears in the presence of God for us. Oh, the diligence of our enemy! Oh, the diligence of our Friend! The one is against us, the other for us, and that continually—"If any man sin, we have an Advocate with the Father, Jesus Christ the righteous."

There are three things in judgment that a lawyer must take heed of: one is the nature of the offense, the other is the meaning and intention of the lawmakers, and a third is to plead for those who are in danger, without respect to affection or reward. And this is the excellency of our Advocate: He will not, cannot be biased to turn aside from doing judgment.... "The just LORD...one that will not do iniquity"—that is, no unrighteousness in judgment (Zeph. 3:5). He will not be provoked to do it, neither by the continual solicitations of your enemy, nor by your continual provocations caused by your infirm condition that might often tempt Him to do it.

Now...Jesus Christ is righteous, and...He pleads for us by the new law, with which Satan has nothing to do, nor, even if he had, can he by it bring in a plea against us because that law, in the very body of it, consists in free promises of giving grace to us and of an everlasting forgiveness of our sin (Jer. 31:31–34; Ezek. 36:25–30; Heb. 8:8–13). O children, your Advocate will stick to the law, to the new law, to the new and everlasting covenant, and will not admit that anything should be pleaded by our foe that is inconsistent with the promise of the gift of grace and of the remission of all sin. This, therefore, is another privilege that those who have Jesus Christ to be their Advocate are made partakers of. He is just, He is righteous,...He will not be turned aside to judge awry, either of the crime or the law, for favor or affection. Nor is there any sin but what is pardonable committed by those who have chosen Jesus Christ to be their Advocate.

Another...advantage that they have who have Jesus Christ to be their Advocate is this: The Father has made Him, even Him who is your Advocate, the umpire and judge in all matters that have, do, or shall fall out between Him and us. Mark this well: For when the Judge Himself, the Judge of the nature of the crime for which I am accused and of matter of law by which I am accused, will be my Advocate—to wit, whether it is in force against me to condemnation or whether by the law of grace I am set free, especially since my Advocate has espoused my cause, promised me deliverance, and pleaded my right to the state of eternal life—must it not go well with me...? It was a great thing that happened to Israel when Joseph became their advocate and when Pharaoh had made him a judge. "Thou," Pharaoh said to Joseph, "shalt be over my house, and according unto thy word shall all my people be ruled. See, I have set thee over all the land of Egypt—and without thee shall no man lift up his hand or foot in all the land of Egypt—only in the throne will I be greater than thou" (Gen. 41:40–44).

What do you say, poor heart, to this? The Judge—to wit, the God of heaven—has become your Advocate, arbitrator in your business; He is to judge. God has referred the matter to Christ, and He has a concern in your concern, an interest in your good prosperity. Christian man, do you hear? You have put your cause into the hand of Jesus Christ and have chosen Him to be your Advocate to plead for you before God and against your adversary.... Are you also willing that He should decide the matter? Can you say unto him as David said, "Judge me, O God, and plead my cause" (Ps. 43:1)? Oh, the care of God toward His people and the desire of their welfare! He has provided them an Advocate, and He has referred all causes and things that may by Satan be objected and brought in against us, to the judgment and sentence of Christ our Advocate.

2

The Physician Who Cures Gets Himself a Name and Begets Encouragement in the Minds of Diseased Folk

By curing the most desperate first, the physician not only earns himself a name, but he also encourages other diseased folk to come to him for help. Hence, you read of our Lord that after, through His tender mercy, He had cured many of great diseases, His fame was spread abroad: "They brought unto him all sick people that were taken with divers diseases and torments, and those which were possessed with devils, and those which were lunatic, and those that had the palsy, and he healed them. And there followed him great multitudes of people from Galilee, and from Decapolis, and from Jerusalem, and from Judea, and from beyond Jordan" (Matt. 4:24–25). See here, He first, by working, gets Himself a fame, a name, and renown; and now men take encouragement, and bring their diseased to Him from all quarters, being helped by what they had heard to believe that their diseased should be healed.

Now as He did with those outward cures, so He does in the offer of His grace and mercy. He offers

From *The Jerusalem Sinner Saved*, in *Works*, 1:76–78.

first to the biggest sinners, that others may take heart to come to Him to be saved.... But why did He do all this? "That in the ages to come he might show the exceeding riches of his grace in his kindness towards us through Christ Jesus" (Eph. 2:7). See, here is a design: God lets out His mercy to great sinners by... design, even to show to the ages to come the exceeding riches of His grace, in His kindness to them through Christ Jesus.

For this reason,...in saving sinners,...He had a design to provoke others to come to Him for mercy. So the same design is here set on foot again, in His calling and converting these...sinners, "that in the ages to come he might show the exceeding riches of his grace," says Paul, "in his kindness towards us through Christ Jesus." There is yet one hint behind. It is said that God saved these "for his great love"; that is, as I think, for the setting forth, for the commendation of His love, for the advance of His love in the hearts and minds of them that should come after. As who should say, God has had mercy upon and been gracious to you that He might show to others, for their encouragement, that they have ground to come to Him to be saved. When God saves one great sinner, it is to encourage another great sinner to come to Him for mercy.

He saved the thief to encourage thieves to come to Him for mercy; He saved Magdalene to encourage other Magdalenes to come to Him for mercy; He saved Saul to encourage Sauls to come to Him for mercy, and Paul himself says this: "For this cause," says he, "I obtained mercy, that in me first Jesus Christ might show forth all long-suffering, for a pattern to them which should hereafter believe on him to life everlasting" (1 Tim. 1:16). How plain are the words! Christ, in saving [Paul], has given to the world a pattern of His grace, that they might see and believe and come and be saved, that they who are to be born hereafter might believe on Jesus Christ to life everlasting.

But what was Paul? Why, he tells you himself: "I am," says he," the chief of sinners." "I was," says he, "a blasphemer, a persecutor, an injurious person; but I obtained mercy" (1 Tim. 1:13). Yes, that is well for you, Paul, but what advantage do we have because of that? "Oh, very much," says he: "For this cause I obtained mercy, that in me first Jesus Christ might show forth all long-suffering, for a pattern to them which should hereafter believe on him to life everlasting" (v. 16).... Jesus Christ would have mercy offered, in the first place, to the biggest sinners because, by their forgiveness and salvation, others, hearing of it, will be encouraged the more to come to Him for mercy. It may well, therefore, be said to God, "Thou delightest in mercy, and mercy pleases Thee" (Mic. 7:18).

Christ Jesus will not miss in His design of offering mercy, in the first place, to the biggest sinners. You know what work the Lord, by laying hold of the woman of Samaria, made among the people there. They knew that she was a town sinner, an adulteress, even one who, in the most audacious manner, lived in uncleanness with a man who was not her husband. But when she, after a turn of her heart, went into the city and said to her neighbors, "Come"—oh, how they came! How they flocked out of the city to Jesus Christ! Then they went out of the city and came to Him. "And many of the Samaritans of that city [people, perhaps, as bad as herself] believed on him for the saying of the woman, which testified, He told me all that ever I did" (John 4:39). That word, "He told me all that ever I did," was a great argument with them, for by that they gathered that though He knew her to be vile, He did not despise her or refuse to show how willing He was to communicate His grace to her; and this fetched over first her, then them.

I once heard a story from a soldier who...had laid siege against a fort, that so long as the besieged were persuaded their foes would show them no favor, they fought like madmen. But when they saw one of their fellows taken and received with favor, they all came tumbling down from their fortress and delivered themselves into their enemies' hands. I am persuaded that if men believed that there is that grace and willingness in the heart of Christ to save sinners, as the Word imports there is, they would come tumbling into His arms. But Satan has blinded their minds so that they cannot see this thing. Nevertheless, the Lord Jesus has, as I said, that others might take heart and come to Him, given out a commandment that mercy should, in the first place, be offered to the biggest sinners. "Begin," says He, "at Jerusalem."[1]

---

1. *The Jerusalem Sinner Saved* is Bunyan's extended exposition of Luke 24:47. Bunyan uses the "Jerusalem sinner" as an extended metaphor throughout the treatise as a great sinner who needs to come to Christ for mercy.

3

Things Related to the Promises of Christ Our Advocate

There are many things relating to the promises, as to the largeness and narrowness of words, as to the freeness and conditionality of them, that we are not able so well to understand, and, therefore, when Satan deals with us about them, we quickly fall to the ground before him. We often conclude that the words of the promise are too narrow and rigid to comprehend; we also truly think that the conditions of some promises do utterly shut us out from hope of justification and life. But our Advocate, who is for us with the Father, He is better acquainted with and learned in this law than to be baffled out with a bold word or two or with a subtle piece of hellish sophistication (Isa. 50:4). He knows the true purport, intent, meaning, and sense of every promise and piece of promise that is in the whole Bible. He can tell how to plead it for advantage against our accuser, and He does so. And I gather it not only from His contest with Satan for Joshua (Zech. 3) and from His conflict with him in the wilderness (Matt. 4) and in heaven (Rev. 14), but also from the practice of Satan's emissaries here; for what his angels do, he also does.

From *The Work of Jesus Christ as an Advocate*, in *Works*, 1:184–86.

Now there is here nothing more apparent than that the instruments of Satan do plead against the church, from the pretended intricacy, ambiguity, and difficulty of the promise, so I gather Satan also does this before the tribunal of God. But there we have one to match him; "we have an Advocate with the Father" who knows law and judgment better than Satan and statute and commandment better than all his angels. And by the verdict of our Advocate, all the words and limits and extensions of words with all conditions of the promises are expounded and applied!

There are many other things relating to our lives that serve our accuser with occasions to make many objections against our salvation, for, besides our daily infirmities, there are in our lives gross sins, many horrible backslidings. Also we often suck and drink in many abominable errors and deceitful opinions, all of which Satan accuses us before the judgment seat of God and pleads hard that we may be damned forever for them. Besides, some of these things are done after light received, against present convictions and dissuasions to the contrary, against solemn engagements to amendment when the bonds of love were upon us (Jer. 2:20). These are crying sins; they have a loud voice in themselves against us and give to Satan great advantage and boldness to sue for our destruction before the bar of God. Nor does Satan lack skill to aggravate and to comment profoundly upon all occasions and circumstances that did attend us in our miscarriages—to wit, that we did it without a cause. Also, had we had grace to have used them, we had many things to help us against such sins and to keep us clean and upright. "There is a sin unto death" (1 John 5:16), and he can tell how to labor by argument and cunning speech to make our transgressions not only to border upon, but to appear in the hue, shape, and figure of that and based on that make his objection against our salvation.... But there he meets with Jesus Christ, our Lord and Advocate, who enters His plea against him, unravels all his reasons and arguments against us, and shows the guile and falsehood of them.

He...also pleads as to the nature of sin, as also to all those high aggravations, and proves that neither the sin in itself, nor yet as joined with all its advantageous circumstances, can be the sin unto death (Col. 2:19), because we hold the head and have not "made shipwreck" of faith (1 Tim. 1:19). But still, as David and Solomon did, we confess and are sorry for our sins. Thus, though we seem through our falls to come short of the promise with Peter (Heb. 4:1–3), and leave our transgressions as stumbling blocks to the world with Solomon, and minister occasion of a question of our salvation among the godly, yet our Advocate fetches us off before God. And we will be found safe and in heaven at last by them in the next world who were afraid they had lost us in this.

But all these points must be managed by Christ for us, against Satan, as a lawyer, an advocate, who to that end now appears in the presence of God for us and wisely handles the very crisis of the word and of the failings of His people together with all those nice and critical juggles by which our adversary labors to bring us down, to the confusion of his face.

But, Satan, here is also sufficient matter for a plea for our Advocate against you. For as much as the next words distinguish between drawing back, and drawing back "unto perdition," every one that draws back does not draw back unto perdition (Heb. 10:38–39). Some of them draw back from, and some in the profession of, the gospel. Judas drew back *from*, and Peter *in* the profession of his faith; for that reason Judas perishes but Peter turns again, because Judas drew back unto perdition, but Peter yet believed to the saving of the soul. Nor does Jesus Christ, when He sees it is to no effect, at any time step in to endeavor to save the soul. Because of this Christ turns Judas over to Satan for his backsliding from the faith and leaves him in Satan's hand, saying, "When he shall be judged, let him be condemned: and let his prayer become sin" (Ps. 109:7). But Christ will not serve Peter so—"The LORD will not leave him in his hand, nor condemn him when he is judged" (Ps. 37:33). He will pray for him before and plead for him after he has been in the temptation and so secure him by virtue of His advocation from the sting and lash of the threatening that is made against final apostasy.

Bronze Door, Bunyan Meeting Church, Bedford

Scenes from *Pilgrim's Progress* are depicted on the bronze doors of the Bunyan Meeting Church. The doors were a gift from Hastings, 9th Duke of Bedford, in 1876.

4

Concerning Christ's Sacrifice

1. The sacrifice, before it was offered, was to have all the sins of the children of Israel confessed over it to signify that Jesus Christ must bear the sins of all His children by covenant....

2. [The sacrifice] must be taken to the place appointed—namely without the camp of Israel—to signify that Jesus Christ must be led to Mount Calvary.

3. The sacrifice was to be killed there to signify that Jesus Christ must and did suffer with the city of Jerusalem for our salvation.

4. The sacrifice must not only have its life taken away, but also some of its flesh burned upon the altar to signify that Jesus Christ... should undergo the pains and torments of the damned in hell.

5. Sometimes there must be a living offering and a dead offering, as the goat that was killed and the scapegoat, the dead bird and the living bird, to signify that Jesus Christ must die and come to life again.

From *The Law and Grace Unfolded*, in *Works*, 1:528–32.

Concerning Christ's Sacrifice

6. The goat that was to die was to be the sin offering, that is, to be offered as the rest of the sin offerings, to make an atonement as a type;...to signify that Christ's death was to make satisfaction for sin and His coming to life again was to bring everlasting justification from the power, curse, and destroying nature of sin.

7. The scapegoat was to be carried by a fit man into the wilderness to signify that Jesus Christ should be both fit and able to carry our sins quite away from us so as they should never be laid to our charge again. Here is grace.

8. The sacrifices under the law, commonly part of them must be eaten to signify that they who are saved should spiritually feed on the body and blood of Jesus Christ or else they have no life by Him.

9. This sacrifice must be eaten with unleavened bread to signify that those who love their sins, that devilish leaven of wickedness, do not feed on Christ.

This is the sum, that there is a sacrifice under the new covenant as there were sacrifices under the old, and that this sacrifice did every way answer that, or those. Indeed, they did suffer for sin in show, but He really; they as the shadow, but He as the substance.

5

Concerning Eternal Security

And though I was thus troubled and tossed and afflicted with the sight and sense of terror of my own wickedness, yet I was afraid to let this sight and sense go quite off my mind. For I found that unless guilt of conscience was taken off the right way, that, by the blood of Christ, a man grew rather worse for the loss of his trouble of mind, than better.... Lord, let it not go off my heart but the right way, but by the blood of Christ, and by the application of Thy mercy through Him to my soul; for that the Scripture lay much upon me: "Without shedding of blood there is no remission" (Heb. 9:22)....

I conceived a falling from and an absolute denial of the gospel of remission of sins by Christ, for from them the apostle begins his argument (Heb. 6:1–3). Secondly, I found that this falling away must be openly, even in the view of the world, even so as to put Christ to an open shame. Thirdly, I found that those He there intended were forever shut up of God both in blindness, hardness, and impenitency: It is impossible they should be renewed again unto repentance. By all these particulars, I found, to God's everlasting praise, my sin was not the sin in this place intended.

From *Grace Abounding to the Chief of Sinners*, in *Works*, 1:16, 85.

Concerning Eternal Security

First, I confessed I was fallen, but not fallen away—that is from the profession of faith in Jesus unto eternal life.

Secondly, I confessed that I had put Jesus Christ to shame by my sin, but not to open shame. I did not deny Him before men nor condemn Him as a fruitless one before the world.

Thirdly, nor did I find that God had shut me up or denied me to come, though I found it hard work indeed to come to Him by sorrow and repentance. Blessed be God for unsearchable grace.

6

Concerning Christ's Blood — Our Only Plea

There is, in some kind, a harmony between His being a sacrifice, a priest, and an advocate. As a sacrifice, our sins were laid upon Him (Isa. 53). As a priest, He bears them (Ex. 28:38). And as an advocate, He acknowledges them to be His own (Ps. 69:5). Now, having acknowledged them to be His own, the quarrel is no more between us and Satan, for the Lord Jesus has espoused our quarrel and made it His. All then that we in this matter have to do is to stand at the bar by faith among the angels and see how the business goes. O blessed God! What a lover of mankind art Thou! And how gracious is our Lord Jesus in His thus managing our matters for us.

Christ pleads the value and virtue of the price of His blood and sacrifice for us.... Therefore, I say, He is concerned with us; His credit, His honor, His glory, and renown lie all away, if those for whom He pleads as an advocate perish for want of worth in His sacrifice pleaded. But will this ever be said of Christ? Or will it be found that any for whom Christ as advocate pleads yet perish for want of worth in the price or of neglect in the advocate to plead it? No, no; He

From *The Work of Jesus Christ as an Advocate*, in *Works*, 1:161, 177.

Concerning Christ's Blood

Himself is concerned, as to His own reputation and honor and as to the value and virtue of His blood, nor will He lose these for want of pleading for them concerned in this office.

SECTION TWO

Christ Jesus the Merciful Savior

Christian's Burden Falls Off

In *Pilgrim's Progress* Bunyan writes, "As Christian came up with the cross, his burden loosened...and fell from off his back, and began to tumble,...till it came to the mouth of the sepulchre, where it fell in, and I saw it no more."

7

Christ's Mercy Offered to the Biggest Sinners Redounds Most to the Fame of His Name

Christ's mercy offered...to the biggest sinners... *redounds most to the fame of His name.*

Christ Jesus, as you may perceive, has called Himself a physician, a doctor for curing diseases, and you know that applause and fame are things that physicians much desire. That helps them with patients, and that also will help their patients to commit themselves to their skill for cure with more confidence and repose of spirit. And the best way for a doctor or physician to get himself a name is, in the first place, to take in hand and cure some patients that all others have given up for lost and dead. Physicians get neither name nor fame by draining of sores or picking out thistles or by laying of bandages to the scratch of a pin; every old woman can do this. But if they would have a name and fame, if they will have it quickly, they must, as I said, do some great and desperate cures. Let them fetch one to life who was dead; let them recover one to his wits who was mad; let them make one who was born blind to see; or let them give ripe wits to a fool. These are notable

From *The Jerusalem Sinner Saved*, in *Works*, 1:75–76.

cures, and he that can do these things, and if he does them first, he will have the name and fame he desires; he may lie in bed till noon.

But we will follow...a...metaphor. Christ...has put Himself under the term of a physician; consequently, He desires that His fame as to the salvation of sinners may spread abroad, that the world may see what He can do. And to this end, He has not only commanded that the biggest sinners should have the first offer of His mercy, but has, as physicians do, put out His bills and published His doings that things may be read and talked of. He has, moreover, in these His blessed bills—the Holy Scriptures, I mean— inserted the very names of persons, the places of their abode, and the great cures that, by the means of His salvation, He has brought upon them to this very end. Here is such a one, who by My grace and redeeming blood was made a monument of everlasting life and such a one who, by My perfect obedience, became an heir of glory. And then He lists their names. *Item*: I saved Lot from the guilt and damnation that he had procured for himself by his incest. *Item*: I saved David from the vengeance that belonged to him for committing adultery and murder. Here is also Solomon, Manasseh, Peter, Magdalene, and many others.... And it is observable, as I said before, we have but very little of the salvation of little sinners mentioned in God's Book, because that would not have answered the design, to wit, to bring glory and fame to the name of the Son of God.

When Christ was crucified and hanged up between the earth and heavens, there were two thieves crucified with Him, and, behold, He lays hold of one of them and will have him away with Him to glory. Was not this a strange act and a display of unthought-of grace? Were there none but thieves there, or were the rest of that company out of His reach? Could He not, do you think, have stooped from the cross to the ground and have laid hold on some more honest man, if He would? Yes, doubtless. Oh! But then He would not have displayed His grace or so have pursued His own designs, namely, to get for Himself a praise and a name. But now He has done it to purpose, so that those who will read this story must confess that the Son of God is full of grace. He left behind proof of the riches thereof when, upon the cross, He took the thief away with Him to glory. Nor can this one act of His be buried; it will be talked of to the end of the world, to His praise. "Men shall speak of the might of thy terrible acts; and I will declare thy greatness. They shall abundantly utter the memory of thy great goodness, and shall sing of thy righteousness.... They shall speak of the glory of thy kingdom, and talk of thy power; to make known to the sons of men his mighty acts, and the glorious majesty of his kingdom" (Ps. 145:6, 12).

When the Word of God came among the conjurors and those soothsayers that you read of (Acts 19) and had prevailed with some of them to accept the grace of Christ, the Holy Ghost records it with a boast, for that it would redound to His praise, saying, "Many of them also which used curious arts brought their books together, and burned them before all men; and they counted the price of them, and found it fifty thousand pieces of silver. So mightily grew the Word of God, and prevailed" (Acts 19:19–20).

It wrenched out of the clutches of Satan some of those of whom he thought himself most sure. "So mightily grew the Word of God." It grew mightily; it encroached upon the kingdom of the Devil. It pursued him and took the prey; it forced him to let go his hold! It brought away captive, as prisoners taken by force of arms, some of the most valiant of his army. It fetched back from, as it were, the confines of hell some of those that were his most trusty who had been at an agreement with hell. It made them come and confess their deeds and burn their books before all men. "So mightily grew the Word of God, and prevailed." Therefore, you see why Christ will have offered mercy, in the first place, to the biggest sinners; they have most need thereof; and this is the most ready way to extol His name "that rideth upon the heavens" to our help.

8

Christ's Offer of Mercy

Jesus Christ would have mercy offered, in the first place, to the biggest sinners, because *that is the way, if they receive it, most to weaken the kingdom of Satan and to keep it lowest in every age of the world.*

The biggest sinners are Satan's colonels and captains, the leaders of his people, and they that most stoutly make head against the Son of God. So let these first be conquered, and his kingdom will be weak. When Ishbosheth had lost his Abner, the kingdom became weak, and he sat tottering then upon his throne. So when Satan loses his strong men, those who are mighty to work iniquity and dexterous to manage others in the same, then is his kingdom weak (2 Sam. 3). Therefore, I say, Christ does not offer mercy in the first place to such, the more to weaken his kingdom. Christ Jesus was glad to see Satan fall like lightning from heaven, that is, suddenly, or headlong, and it was, surely, by casting of him out of strong possession and by recovering of some notorious sinners out of his clutches (Luke 10:17–19).

Samson, when he would pull down the Philistines' temple, took hold of the two main pillars of it,

---

From *The Jerusalem Sinner Saved*, in *Works*, 1:78–79.

and, breaking them, down came the house. Christ came to destroy the works of the Devil and to destroy by converting grace as well as by redeeming blood. Now, sin swarms and flesh lies by legions and whole armies in the souls of the biggest sinners as in garrisons; therefore, the most direct way to destroy it is first to deal with such sinners by the word of the gospel and by the merits of His passion.

I speak by experience. I was one of these... great sin-breeders; I infected all the youth of the town where I was born with all manner of youthful vanities. The neighbors counted me so, my practice proved me so, and this is the reason Christ Jesus took me first. And taking me first, the contagion was much allayed all over the town. When God made me sigh, they would hearken and inquiringly say, "What's the matter with John?" They also gave various opinions of me, but, as I said, sin cooled and failed as to his full career. When I went out to seek the bread of life, some of them would follow, and the rest were put into deep thought at home. At first, almost the whole town at times would go out to hear at the place where I found good; young and old for a while had some reformation on them. Also, some of them, perceiving that God had mercy upon me, came crying to Him for mercy too.

And do you not think now that if God would but take hold of the hearts of some of the most notorious in your town, in your family, or country, that this thing would be verified before your faces? It would, it would, to the joy of you who are godly, to the making of hell to sigh, to the great suppressing of sin, the glory of Christ, and the joy of angels of God. And ministers should, therefore, that this work might go on, take advantages to persuade the biggest sinners to come in to Christ, according to my text and their commission, "beginning at Jerusalem."

9

Encouragement to the Unbeliever Not to Despair

Would Jesus Christ have mercy offered, in the first place, to the biggest sinners? Then *this shows how unreasonable a thing it is for men to despair of mercy*; for those that presume, I shall say something to them afterward.

I now speak to those who despair. There are four sorts of despair. There is the despair of devils; there is the despair of souls in hell; there is the despair that is grounded upon men's deficiency; and there is the despair that they are perplexed with that are willing to be saved but are too strongly borne down with the burden of their sins.

The despair of devils, the damned's despair, and that despair that a man has of attaining life because of his own deficiency are all reasonable. Why should not devils and damned souls despair? Why should not man despair of getting to heaven by his own abilities? I, therefore, am concerned only with the fourth sort of despair, to wit, with the despair of those who want to be saved but are too strongly borne down with the burden of their sins. I say, therefore, to you who are like this, "Why do you despair?"

From *The Jerusalem Sinner Saved*, in *Works*, 1:91–92.

Encouragement to the Unbeliever 89

But, for the first, you are still in the land of the living; and, for the second, you have ground to believe quite the contrary. Christ is able to save to the uttermost those that come to God by Him. And if He were not willing, He would not have commanded that mercy, in the first place, should be offered to the biggest sinners. Besides, He has said, "And let him that is athirst come. And whosoever will, let him take the water of life freely," that is, *with all my heart*. What ground now is here for despair? If you say, "The number and burden of my sins," I answer, "No, that is rather a ground for faith because such a one, above all others, is invited by Christ to come unto Him and is even promised rest and forgiveness if they come" (Matt. 11:28). What grounds, then, do you have to despair?

Your desires to be saved by Christ have put you under a…promise, so there is that…to hold you up in hope, though your present burden be never so heavy (Matt. 5:3, 6). As for what you say about God's silence to you, perhaps He has spoken to you once or twice already, but you have not perceived it (Job 33:14–15).… What if God is silent to you—is that grounds for despair? Not at all, so long as there is a promise in the Bible that God will in no wise cast away the coming sinner and so long as He invites the Jerusalem sinner to come unto Him (John 6:37).

Do not build…despair upon these things; they are no sufficient foundation for it, with so many promises being in the Bible and such a discovery of His mercy to great sinners of old. This is especially true since we also have a clause in the commission given to ministers to preach, that they should begin with the Jerusalem sinners in their offering of mercy to the world.

Despair!... For shame, forbear; let them despair who dwell where there is no God and are confined to those chambers of death that cannot be reached by any redemption. A living man despairs when he is chided for murmuring and complaining! (Lam. 3:39). Oh! So long as we are where promises swarm, where mercy is proclaimed, where grace reigns, and where Jerusalem sinners are privileged with the first offer of mercy, it is a base thing to despair. Despair undervalues the promise, undervalues the invitation, undervalues the proffer of grace. Despair undervalues the ability of God the Father and the redeeming blood of Christ His Son. Oh, unreasonable despair!

Besides, I am persuaded also that despair is the cause that there are so many who are eager to be atheists in the world. Because they have entertained a conceit that God will never be merciful to them, they labor to persuade themselves that there is no God at all, as if their misbelief would kill God or cause Him to cease to be. A poor shift for an immortal soul, for a soul who does not like to retain God in its knowledge! If this be the best that despair can do, let it go, man, and take yourself to faith, to prayer, to wait for God, and to hope, in spite of ten thousand doubts. And for your encouragement, take yet, as an addition to what has already been said, the following Scripture: "The LORD taketh pleasure in them that fear him, in those that hope in his mercy" (Ps. 147:11).

"O fools, and slow of heart to believe all that the prophets have spoken!" (Luke 24:25). Mark you, here, slowness to believe is a piece of folly. Yes, but

Encouragement to the Unbeliever 91

you say, "I do believe some, and I believe what can make against me." Yes, but sinner, Christ Jesus here calls you a fool for not believing all. Believe all, and despair if you can! He who believes all believes that text that says Christ would have mercy preached first to the Jerusalem sinners. He who believes all believes all the promises and consolations of the Word; and the promises and consolations of the Word weigh heavier than do all the curses and threatenings of the law, and mercy rejoices against judgment. So believe all, and mercy will, to your conscience, weigh judgment down and so minister comfort to your soul. "The LORD take the yoke off your jaws, since He has set meat before you" (Hos. 11:4). And it will help you to remember that He is pleased, in the first place, to offer mercy to the biggest sinners.

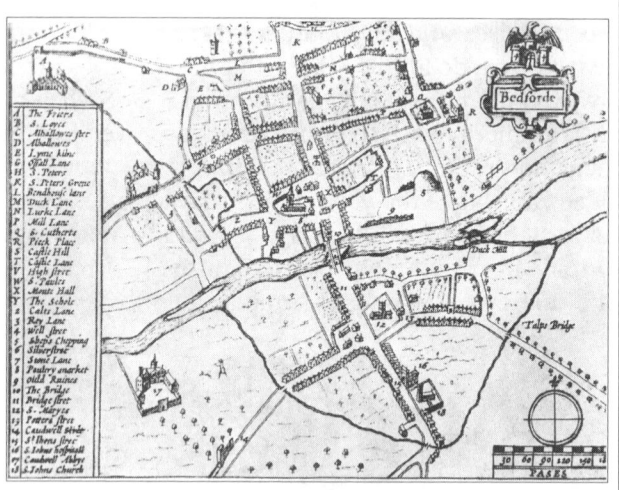

John Speed's Map of Bedfordshire

John Speed (1542–1629) was a cartographer who made county maps that often showed town plans. His 1611 map of Bedford includes sites such as St. John's Church and the town bridge.

10

Mercy Offered to All Sinners—Great or Small!

Would Jesus Christ have mercy offered, in the first place, to the biggest sinners? Then here is ground for those who, as to practice, have not been such to come to Him for mercy.

Although there is no sin little of itself, because it is a contradiction of the nature and majesty of God, yet we must admit of divers numbers and also of aggravations. Two sins are not as many as three, nor are three that are done in ignorance as big as one that is done against light, against knowledge and conscience. Also, there is the child in sin, and a man in sin that has his hairs gray and his skin wrinkled for very age. And we must put a difference between these sinners also, for can it be that a child of seven or ten or sixteen years old should be such a sinner— a sinner so vile in the eyes of the law as he who has walked according to the course of this world forty, fifty, sixty, or seventy years? Now, the youth, this boy, though he is a sinner, is but a little sinner when compared with such. Now, I say, if there be room for the first sort, for those of the biggest size, certainly there is room for the lesser size. If there be a door

From *The Jerusalem Sinner Saved*, in *Works*, 1:94–95.

wide enough for a giant to go in at, there is certainly room for a dwarf. If Christ Jesus has grace enough to save great sinners, He has surely grace enough to save little ones. If he can forgive five hundred pence, for certain he can forgive fifty (Luke 7:41–42).

A sinner may be comparatively a little sinner and sensibly a great one. There are, then, two sorts of greatness in sin—greatness by reason of number and greatness by reason of thoroughness of conviction of the horrible nature of sin. In this last sense, he that has but one sin, if such a one could be found, may, in his own eyes, find himself the biggest sinner in the world. Let this man or this child, therefore, put himself among the great sinners and plead with God as great sinners do, and let him expect to be saved with the great sinners as soon and as heartily as they. And a little sinner who, comparatively, is truly so, if he will graciously give way to conviction and will, in God's light, diligently weigh the horrible nature of his own sin, may yet sooner obtain forgiveness for them at the hands of the heavenly Father than he that has ten times his sins, and so cause to cry ten times harder to God for mercy.

For the grievousness of the cry is a great thing with God, for if He will hear the widow if she cries at all, how much more if she cries most grievously? (Ex. 22:22–23). It is not the number but the true sense of the abominable nature of sin that makes the cry for pardon lamentable. He, as I said, who has many sins may not cry so loud in the ears of God as he who has far fewer; he, in our present sense, who is in his own eyes the biggest sinner is he who soonest finds mercy. The offer, then, is to the biggest

Mercy Offered to All Sinners

sinner—to the biggest sinner first, and the mercy is first obtained by him who first confesses himself to be such a one.

There are men who strive at the throne of grace for mercy by pleading the greatness of their necessity. Now their plea, as to the prevalence of it, lies not in their counting up of the number, but in the sense of the greatness of their sins and in the vehemence of their cry for pardon. And it is observable that though the birthright was Reuben's and, for his foolishness, given to the sons of Joseph, yet Judah prevailed above his brethren, and of him came the Messiah (1 Chron. 5:1–2). There is a heavenly subtlety to be managed in this matter. "Thy brother came with subtilty, and hath taken away thy blessing".... The offer is to the biggest sinner, to the biggest sinner first, but if he refrains from crying, the sinner that is a sinner less by far than he, both as to number and the nature of transgression, may get the blessing first, if he shall have grace to cry loudly and well. For the loudest cry is heard furthest, and the most lamentable pierces soonest.

Little sinner! When you go to God—though you know in your conscience that you, as to acts, are no thief, no murderer, no whore, no liar, no false swearer, or the like, and in reason must needs understand that thus you are not so profanely vile as others—yet when you go to God for mercy, know no man's sins but your own, make mention of no man's sins but your own. Also labor not to lessen your own, but magnify and greaten them by all just circumstances and be as if there was never a sinner in the world but yourself. Also, cry out as if you were but the only undone man, and that is the way to obtain God's mercy.

It is one of the loveliest sights in the world to see a little sinner commenting upon the greatness of his sins, multiplying and multiplying them to himself till he makes them in his own eyes bigger and higher than he sees any other man's sins to be in the world. And as base a thing it is to see a man do otherwise, and as basely will come on it (Luke 18:10–14). As, therefore, I said to the great sinner before, let him take heed lest he presume; I say now to the little sinner, let him take heed not to hide the reality of his sins. For there is as great an aptness in the little sinner to hide sin as there is in the great one. "He that covereth his sins shall not prosper," be he a sinner little or great (Prov. 28:13).

11

What Is Meant by This "Water of Life"?

By this term *water*, an opposition to sin is presented to us. Sin is compared to water, to deadly waters, and man is said to drink it as one who drinks water. "How much more abominable and filthy is man, which drinketh iniquity like water?" (Job 15:16). So, then, that grace and the Spirit of grace is compared to water to show what an antidote grace is against sin. It is, as I may call it, counterpoison to it. It is that *only* thing by the virtue of which sin can be forgiven, vanquished, and overcome.

By this term *water*, you have an opposition also to the curse that is due to sin presented to you. The curse is compared to water; the remedy is compared to water. Let the curse come into the bowels of the damned, says the psalmist, like water (Ps. 109:18). The grace of God also, as you see, is compared to water. The curse is burning; water is cooling. The curse burns with hellfire; cooling is by the grace of the holy gospel. But they that overstand the day of grace will not be able to cool their tongues with the

---

From *The Water of Life, or A Discourse Showing the Richness and Glory of the Grace and Spirit of the Gospel, as Set Forth in Scripture by This Term*, The Water of Life, in *Works*, 3:541–42.

amount of this water that would hang on the tip of one's finger (Luke 16:24–25).

Water is also of a spreading nature, and so is sin, so sin may for this also be compared to water. It overspreads the whole man and infects every member; it covers all, as does water. Grace for this cause may be also compared to water. For it is of a spreading nature and can, if God will, cover the face of the whole earth, of body and soul.

Sin is of a fouling, defiling nature, and grace is of a washing, cleansing nature. Therefore grace, and the Spirit of grace, is compared to water. "I will," says God, "sprinkle clean water upon you, and ye shall be clean: from all your filthiness, and from all your idols, will I cleanse you" (Ezek. 36:25).

Water—the element of water naturally descends to and abides in low places, in valleys and places that are undermost, and the grace of God and the Spirit of grace are of that nature also. The hills and lofty mountains have not the rivers running over the tops of them, though they may run among them. But they run among the valleys, and "God resisteth the proud, and giveth grace to the humble," [and] "to the lowly" (John 4:6; 1 Peter 5:5; Prov. 3:34).

The grace of God is compared to water, for that is what causes fruitfulness; water causes fruitfulness, and want of water is the cause of barrenness. This is the reason why the whole world is so empty of fruit to Godward, even because so few of the children of men have the Spirit of grace in their hearts.

As there is a great special significance in this term *water*, so there is in this term *life*, water of life. "He showed me the water of life." In that, therefore, there is added to this word *water*, that of *life*; it is, in the general sense, to show what excellent virtue and operation there is in this water. It is *aquae vitae*, water of life, or water that has a health and life in it.

It also shows us that there is not anything in the world or in the doctrine of the world, the law, that can make them live. Life is only in this water; death is in all other things. The law, I say, which is that that would, if anything in the whole world, give life unto the world, but that yet kills, condemns, and was added that the offence might abound. So there is no life either in the world or in the doctrine of the world. It is only in this water, in this grace of God, which is here called the water of life, or God's *aquae vitae*.

It is also called the water of life to show that by the grace of God men may live, however dead their sins have made them. When God will say to a sinner, "Live," though he be dead in his sins, "he shall live." "I said unto thee when thou wast in thy blood, Live; yea, I said unto thee when thou wast in thy blood, Live" (Ezek. 16:6). And again, "The dead shall hear the voice of the Son of God; and they that hear shall live" (John 5:25). That is, when He speaks words of grace and mixes those words with the Spirit and grace of the gospel, then men will live, for such words so attended, and such words only, are spirit and life. "The words that I speak unto you," says Christ, "they are spirit, and they are life" (John 6:63).

In that this grace of God is here presented unto us under the terms of *water of life*, it is to show that some are sick of that disease that nothing can cure but that. There are many diseases in the world, and there are also remedies for those diseases; but there is a disease that nothing will, can, or shall cure except a sip from this bottle, a draught of this *aquae vitae*, this water of life. This is intimated by the invitation, "Let him take the water of life freely" (Rev. 22:17). And again, "I will give unto him that is athirst of the fountain of the water of life freely" (Rev. 21:6). This is spoken to the sick, to those who are sick with the disease that only Christ, as a physician with His water of life, can cure (Mark 2:17). But few are sick with this disease; few know what it is to be made sick with this disease. There is nothing that can make men sick with this disease but the law and sin, and nothing can cure but the grace of God by the gospel, called here the *water of life*.

SECTION THREE

Hope for Sinners

Bunyan's Cottage at Elstow

An engraving portraying the cottage where Bunyan and his first wife began their married life.

12

A Great Sinner's Encouragement to Come to Christ

But I say, what is this to him who would desire to be saved by Christ? As to greatness, his sins never yet reach to the nature of the sins that the sinners intended by the text had made themselves guilty of [Luke 24:47]. He who would be saved by Christ has an honorable esteem of Him, but those of Jerusalem preferred a murderer before Him. And as for Him, they cried, "Away, away with Him. It is not fit that He should live." Perhaps you will object that you have a thousand times preferred a stinking lust over Him. I answer, "Be it so; it is but what is common to men to do, nor does the Lord Jesus make such a foolish life a bar to you to forbid your coming to Him, or a bond to His grace that it might be kept from you. But He admits of your repentance and offers Himself unto you freely, as you stand among the Jerusalem sinners."

Therefore, take encouragement, man; mercy is, by the text, held forth to the biggest sinners. Put yourself into the number of the worst by reckoning that you may be one of the first and may not be put off till the biggest sinners are served. For the biggest

From *The Jerusalem Sinner Saved*, in *Works*, 1:89–90.

sinners are first invited; consequently, if they come, they are likely to be the first that will be served. It was so with Jerusalem: Jerusalem sinners were first invited, and they did come first—and there came three thousand of them the first day they were invited. How many came afterwards none can tell—they were first served.

Put in your name, man, among the biggest, in case you are made to wait till they are served. You have some men who think themselves very cunning because they put up their names in their prayers among those who feign it, saying, "God, I thank Thee that I am not as bad as the worst." But believe it, if they will be saved at all, they will be saved in the last place. The first in their own eyes will be served last, and the last or worst will be first. The text insinuates it: "Begin at Jerusalem"; and reason backs it, for they have most need. See, therefore, how God's ways are above ours; we are for serving the worst last, but God is for serving the worst first. The man at the pool, that to my thinking was longest in his disease and most helpless as to his cure, was first healed. Indeed, he only was healed; for we read that Christ healed him, but we read not then that He healed one more there (John 5:1–10)! So if you want to be served first, put in your name among the very worst of sinners. Say, when you are upon your knees, "Lord, here is a Jerusalem sinner! A sinner of the biggest size! One whose burden is of the greatest bulk and heaviest weight! One who cannot stand long without sinking into hell without Thy supporting hand! 'Be not thou far from me, O LORD! O my strength, haste thee to help me!'" (Ps. 22:19).

A Great Sinner's Encouragement

I say, put in your name with Magdalene, with Manasseh, that you may experience what the Magdalene and the Manasseh sinners do. The man in the gospel made the desperate condition of his child an argument with Christ to hasten his cure: "Sir, come down," he says, "ere my child die" (John 4:49). And Christ regarded his haste, saying, "Go thy way; thy son liveth" (v. 50). Haste requires haste. David was for speed: "Deliver me speedily"; "Hear me speedily"; "Answer me speedily" (Pss. 31:2; 69:17; 102:2). But why speedily? I am in "the net"; "I am in trouble"; "My days are consumed like smoke" (Pss. 31:4; 69:17; 102:3). Deep calls to deep; necessity calls for help; great necessity for present help. So, I say, be ruled by me in this matter; do not pretend to be another man if you have been a filthy sinner. Instead, go in your colors to Jesus Christ and put yourself among the most vile, and allow Him alone to "put thee among the children" (Jer. 3:19). Confess all that you know of yourself. I know you will find it hard work to do this, especially if your mind is legal, but do it so you will not stay and be deferred with the little sinners until the great ones have had their alms.

I have one thing more to offer for your encouragement, you who call yourself one of the biggest sinners, and that is that you are, as it were, called by name, in the first place, to come in for mercy. You man of Jerusalem, hear the call. Men do so in courts of law and presently cry out, "Here, sire," and then they shoulder and crowd and say, "Please move, for I am called into the court." Why, this is your case, Jerusalem sinner; be of good cheer—He's calling you (Mark 10:46–49). Why are you sitting still?

Arise! Why are you standing still? Come, man, your call should give you authority to come.

Is not this an encouragement to the biggest sinners to make their application to Christ for mercy? "Come unto me, all ye that labour and are heavy laden," also confirms this thing; that is, that the biggest sinner and he that has the biggest burden is he who is first invited. Christ points over the heads of thousands as He sits on the throne of grace, directly to such a man, and He says, "Bring in here the maimed, the halt, and the blind; let the Jerusalem sinner that stands there behind come to Me." Since Christ says, "Come" to you, let the angels make a lane and let all men make room so the Jerusalem sinner may come to Jesus Christ for mercy.

Would Jesus Christ have mercy offered, in the first place, to the biggest sinners? Then *come, you sinful wretch, and let me a little enter into an argument with you.* Why will you not come to Jesus Christ since you are a Jerusalem sinner? How can you find it in your heart to set yourself against grace, against such grace as that which offers mercy to you? What spirit possesses you and holds you back from a sincere closure with your Savior? Behold, God groaningly complains of you, saying, "But Israel would none of me," and, "When I called, none did answer" (Ps. 81:11; Isa. 66:4).

13

Biggest Sinners Have the Most Need of Mercy

He who has most need, reason says, should be helped first. I mean when a helping hand is offered, and now it is; for the gospel of the grace of God is sent to help the world (Acts 16:9). But the biggest sinner has most need. Therefore...when mercy is sent down from heaven to men, the worst of men should have the first offer of it. "Begin at Jerusalem." This is the reason that the Lord Christ Himself gives regarding why, in His lifetime, He left the best and turned to the worst; why He sat so far from the righteous and stuck so close to the wicked. "They that are whole," says He, "have no need of the physician, but they that are sick: I came not to call the righteous, but the sinners to repentance" (Mark 2:17)....

Men who are at the point of death have more need of the physician than those who are only now and then troubled with a heart-fainting qualm. The publicans and sinners were, as it were, in the mouth of death; death was swallowing them down. Therefore, the Lord Jesus receives them first, offers them mercy first. "The whole have no need of the physician, but they that are sick. I came not to call

From *The Jerusalem Sinner Saved*, in *Works*, 1:73–77.

the righteous, but the sinners to repentance." The sick man, as I said, is the biggest sinner, whether he sees his disease or not. He is stained from head to foot, from heart to life and conversation.... This...is the man that has need, most need, and therefore, in reason, should be helped in the first place.... Jerusalem sinners...[are] of the biggest size, and therefore, those who have the greatest need. So they must have mercy offered to them before it be offered anywhere else in the world. "Begin at Jerusalem": offer mercy first to a Jerusalem sinner. This man has most need; he is furthest from God, nearest to hell, and so he is one that has most need. This man's sins are in number the most, in cry the loudest, in weight the heaviest, and, consequently, will sink him soonest, so he has most need of mercy. This man is shut up in Satan's hand, strongly bound in the cords of his sins. He is one that justice is whetting his sword to cut off and, therefore, has most need, not only of mercy, but that it should be extended to him in the first place....

Now where pity and compassion are, there is yearning of bowels; where there is that, there is a readiness to help. And, I say again, the more deplorable and dreadful the condition is, the more directly do bowels and compassion turn themselves to such and offer help and deliverance. All this flows from our first Scripture proof: "I came to call them that have need; I came to call them first, while the rest look on and murmur."

"How shall I give thee up, Ephraim?" Ephraim revolted against God; he was a man who had given himself up to devilism by a company of men, the ten tribes that worshiped devils, while Judah kept with his God. But "how shall I give thee up, Ephraim? *How* shall I deliver thee, Israel? How shall I make thee as Admah? How shall I set thee as Zeboim? (And yet thou art worse than they, nor has Samaria committed half thy sins [Ezek. 16:46–51]). Mine heart is turned within me, my repentings are kindled together" (Hos. 11:8).

But where do you find that ever the Lord did thus roll in His bowels for and after any self-righteous man? No, no, it is the publicans and harlots, idolaters and Jerusalem sinners for whom His bowels thus yearn and tumble about within Him. For, alas!— poor worms, they have most need of mercy.

Had not the Good Samaritan more compassion for that man who fell among thieves (though that fall was occasioned by his going from the place where they worshiped God to Jericho, the cursed city) than he had for any other besides? His wine was for him, his oil was for him, his beast for him; his penny, his care, and his swaddling bands for him. For, alas! wretch, he had most need (Luke 10:30–35).

Zaccheus the publican—the chief of the publicans, one who had made himself the richer by wronging of others—the Lord at that time singled him out from all the rest of his brother publicans, and that in the face of many Pharisees, and proclaimed in the audience of them all that that day salvation had come to his house (Luke 19:1–8).

The woman, also, that had been bound down by Satan for eighteen years together, His compassions putting Him upon it, He freed her even though those who stood by snarled at him for doing so (Luke 13:11–13)....

Mercy seems to be out of its proper channel when it deals with self-righteous men, but then it runs with a full stream when it extends itself to the biggest sinners. As God's mercy is not regulated by man's goodness nor obtained by man's worthiness, so not much is set out by saving of any such.

And here let me ask my reader a question: Suppose that, as you are walking by some pond side, you spy in it four or five children, all in danger of drowning, and one is in more danger than all the rest. How do you judge which has most need to be helped out first? I know you will say, "He that is nearest drowning." Why, this is the case: the bigger sinner, the nearer drowning; therefore, the bigger sinner, the more need of mercy—of help by mercy in the first place. And to this our text agrees when it says, "Beginning at Jerusalem." "Let the Jerusalem sinner," says Christ, "have the first offer, the first invitation, the first tender of My grace and mercy, for he is the biggest sinner and so has most need thereof."

14

God's "Bending" of Men's Hearts

If twenty men were to hear a pardon read, and only one of those twenty were condemned to die, and the pardon was for none but that one, which of these men, do you think, would taste the sweetness of that pardon—those who are not or he who was condemned? The condemned man, doubtless. This is the case in hand. The broken in heart is a condemned man. It is a sense of condemnation, with other things, that has indeed broken his heart, and there is not anything but sense of forgiveness that can bind it up or heal it. But could that heal it, could he not taste, truly taste, or rightly relish this forgiveness? No, forgiveness would be to him as it is to one who does not sense his lack of it.

But, I say, what is the reason some so prize what others so despise since they both stand in need of the same grace and mercy of God in Christ? Why, the one sees and the other sees nothing of this woeful miserable state. And thus have I shown you the necessity of a broken heart:

From *The Acceptable Sacrifice or, The Excellency of a Broken Heart*, in *Works*, 1:708–9. The title page states, "By John Bunyan who died, while this, his last Work, was in the Press." This is Bunyan's exposition of Psalm 51:17.

1. Man is dead and must be quickened.
2. Man is a fool and must be made wise.
3. Man is proud and must be humbled.
4. Man is self-willed and must be broken.
5. Man is fearless and must be made to consider.
6. Man is a false believer and must be rectified.
7. Man is a lover of sin and must be weaned from it.
8. Man is wild and must be tamed.
9. Man disrelishes the things of God and can take no savor in them until his heart is broken....

And thus...I...will...show you why or how it comes to pass that a broken heart, a heart truly contrite, is to God such an excellent thing.... Why it is with God or in His esteem an excellent thing...is shown by what follows.

A broken heart is the handiwork of God—a heart of His own preparing, for His own service. It is a sacrifice of His own providing, of His providing for Himself; as Abraham said in another case, "God will provide himself a lamb" (Gen. 22:8). Because of this it is said, "The preparations of the heart in man are from the Lord." And again, "God maketh my heart soft, and the Almighty troubleth me" (Job 23:16). The heart, as it is by nature hard, stupid, and impenetrable, so it remains, and so will remain until God, as was said, bruises it with His hammer and melts it with His fire. The stony nature of it is therefore said to be taken away by God. "I will take away the stony heart out of your flesh, and I will give you," says He, "a heart of flesh" (Ezek. 36:26). I will take away the stony heart, or the stoniness, or the hardness of your heart, and I will give you a heart of flesh; that is, I will make your heart sensible, soft, wieldable, governable, and penitent. Sometimes He bids men rend their hearts, not because they can, but to convince them rather that though it must be so, they cannot do it. So He bids them make themselves a new heart and a new spirit for the same purpose also, for if God does not rend it, it remains unrent. If God makes it not new, it abides an old one still.

This is what is meant by His bending of men for Himself and of His working in them that which is pleasing in His sight (Zech. 9:13). The heart, soul, or spirit, as in itself, as it came from God's fingers, is a precious thing, a thing in God's account worth more than all the world. This heart, soul, or spirit sin has hardened, the Devil has bewitched, and the world has deceived. This heart, thus beguiled, God covets and desires: "My son," says He, "give me thine heart, and let thine eyes observe my ways" (Prov. 23:26).

Statue of Bunyan

This bronze statue was presented to Bedford by the Duke of Bedford in 1874. Around its pedestal are three bronze panels depicting scenes from *Pilgrim's Progress*.

15

Born of God: A Sermon on John 1:13

Those who believe are born to it, as an heir is to an inheritance—they are born of God, not of flesh, nor of the will of man, but of God; not of blood, that is, not by generation, not born to the kingdom of heaven by the flesh, not because I am the son of a godly man or woman—that is meant by blood (see Acts 17:26). He "hath made of one blood all nations." But when He says here "not of blood," He rejects all carnal privileges they did boast of. They boasted they were Abraham's seed. "No, no," says He, "it is not of blood. Do not think to say that you have Abraham as your father; you must be born of God if you go to the kingdom of heaven.

Men who believe in Jesus Christ to the effectual receiving of Jesus Christ are born to it. He does not say they will be born to it, but they are born to it—born of God unto God and the things of God before he receives God to eternal salvation. "Except a man be born again, he cannot see the kingdom of God." Now, unless he is born of God, he cannot see it. Suppose the kingdom of God be what it will, he cannot

---

From "Mr. Bunyan's Last Sermon; Preached August 19, 1688," in *Works*, 2:755–58. Bunyan preached this sermon two days before he became fatally ill and twelve days before he died.

see it before he is begotten of God.... Believing is the consequence of the new birth; "not of blood, nor of the will of man, but of God."

If a child that is newly born does not have other comforts to keep it warm than it had in its mother's womb, it dies; it needs something for its health and comfort. So Christ had swaddling clothes prepared for Him; so those who are born again must have some promise of Christ to keep them alive. Those who are in a carnal state warm themselves with other things, but those who are born again cannot live without some promise of Christ to keep them alive. Christ did this for the poor infant in Ezekiel 16:8...; and when women are with child, what fine things will they prepare for their child! Oh, but what fine things has Christ prepared to wrap all in who are born again!

When a child is in its mother's lap, the mother takes great delight to have what will be for its comfort. So it is with God's children; they shall be kept on His knee (Isa. 66:11). They shall "suck and be satisfied with the breasts of her consolations"; "As one whom his mother comforteth, so will I comfort you" (v. 13). There is a similarity in these things that nobody knows of but those who are born again.

There is usually some similarity between the father and the child. It may be the child looks like its father; so those that are born again have a new likeness—they have the image of Jesus Christ (Gal. 4). Everyone who is born of God has something of the features of heaven upon him.... Christ describes children of the Devil by their features—the children of the Devil will do his works; all works of unrighteousness are the Devil's works. If you are earthly, you have borne the image of the earthly; if heavenly, you have borne the image of the heavenly.

When a man has a child, he trains him up to his own liking—he learns the custom of his father's house. So are those who are born of God—they have learned the custom of the true church of God; there they learn to cry "my Father" and "my God"; they are brought up in God's house; and they learn the method and form of God's house for regulating their lives in this world.

It is natural for children to depend upon their father for what they want. If they want a pair of shoes, they go and tell him. If they want bread, they go and tell him. So should the children of God do. Do you want spiritual bread? Go tell God. Do you want strength of grace? Ask it of God. Do you want strength against Satan's temptations? Go and tell God. When the Devil tempts you, run home and tell your heavenly Father—go, pour out your complaints to God; this is natural to children. If anyone wrongs them, they go and tell their father; so do those who are born of God. When they meet with temptations, they go and tell God of them.

All God's children are criers—you cannot be quiet without a belly full of the milk of God's Word. You cannot be satisfied without peace with God. Pray you, consider it, and be serious with yourselves; if you have not these marks, you will fall short of the kingdom of God—you will never have an interest there. "There" is no intruding. They will say, "Lord, Lord, open to us," and He will say, "I know you not." No child of God—no heavenly inheritance. We sometimes give something to those who are not our children, but we do not give them our lands. Oh do not flatter yourselves with a portion among the sons unless you live like sons. When we see a king's son play with a beggar, this is unbecoming; so if you are the king's children, live like the king's children. If you are risen with Christ, set your affections on things above and not on things below. When you come together, talk of what your Father promised you; you should all love your Father's will and be content and pleased with the exercises you meet with in the world.

Lastly, if you are the children of God, learn that lesson: Gird up the loins of your mind as obedient children, not fashioning yourselves according to your former conversation, but being holy in all manner of conversation. Consider that the holy God is your Father, and let this oblige you to live like the children of God that you may look your Father in the face, with comfort, another day.

16

The Excellence of a Broken Heart before God

The reason a broken heart is to God such an excellent thing is this: A broken heart prizes Christ and has a high esteem for Him. Those who are whole have no need of a physician, but the sick do; this sick man is the brokenhearted in the text, for God makes men sick by smiting them, by breaking their hearts. For this reason sickness and wounds are put together, for the one is a true effect of the other (Mic. 6:13; Hos. 5:13; Mark 2:17). Can any think that God should be pleased when men despise His Son, saying, "He hath no form nor comeliness, and when we shall see him, there is no beauty that we should desire him" (Isa. 23:2)? And yet those whose hearts God has not softened say this of Him; even the elect themselves confess that before their hearts were broken, they set light by Him also. He is, they say, "despised and rejected of men..., and we hid as it were our faces from him; he was despised, and we esteemed him not" (Isa. 53:3).

He is indeed the great deliverer, but what is a deliverer to those who never saw themselves in bondage, as was said before? So it is said of Him who

From *The Acceptable Sacrifice*, in *Works*, 1:710–11.

delivered the city, "No man remembered that same poor man" (Eccl. 9:15). He has sorely suffered and been bruised for the transgression of man, that they might not receive the sting and hell, which by their sins they have procured to themselves. But what is that to them who never saw anything but beauty and never tasted anything but sweetness in sin? It is he who holds by his intercession the hands of God and that causes Him to forbear to cut off the drunkard, the liar, and unclean person, even when they are in the very act and work of their abomination. But their hard heart, their stupefied heart, has no sense of such kindness as this, and therefore they take no notice of it. How many times has God said to this dresser of His vineyard, "Cut down the barren fig tree," while He yet by His intercession has prevailed for a reprieve for another year! But no notice is taken of this; no thanks is from them returned to Him for such kindness of Christ. Such ungrateful, unthankful, inconsiderate wretches as these must be a continual eyesore, as I may say, and great provocation to God, and yet men will do this before their hearts are broken (Luke 13:6–9).

Christ, as I said, is called a physician; He is the only soul physician. He heals, however desperate the disease may be, and He heals the sick person forever. "I give unto them eternal life," and He does it all free of cost, out of mere mercy and compassion (John 10:28). But what is all this to one who does not see his sickness, who sees nothing of a wound? What is the best physician alive, or all the physicians in the world put together, to him who knows no sickness, who is sensible of no disease? Physicians, as was

The Excellence of a Broken Heart

said, may go begging for all the healthy. Physicians are of no esteem except to the sick or upon a supposition of being so now or at any other time.

Why, this is why Christ is so little set by in the world. God has not made them sick by smiting them. His sword has not given them the wound; His dart has not been struck through their liver; they have not been broken with His hammer or melted with His fire. So they have no regard to His physician, and they slight all the provision that God has made for the salvation of the soul.

But now let such a soul be wounded, let such a man's heart be broken, let such a man be made sick through the sting of guilt and be made to wallow himself in ashes under the burden of his transgressions, and then who but Christ, as has been showed afore. Then the physician; then, "Wash me, Lord"; then "Heal my wounds"; then, "Pour Thy wine and oil into my sore"; then, "Lord Jesus, cause me to hear the voice of joy and gladness, that the bones which Thou hast broken may rejoice." Nothing now is as welcome to him as healing, and so nothing—no man—is as desirable now as Christ. His name to such is the best of names; His love to such is the best of love; Himself being now not only in Himself but also, to such a soul, the chiefest of ten thousand (Song 5:10).

As bread to the hungry, as water to the thirsty, as light to the blind, and as liberty to the imprisoned, so and a thousand times more is Jesus Christ to the wounded and to those who are brokenhearted.

Now, as was said, this must be excellent in God's eyes since Christ Jesus is so glorious in His eyes. To condemn what a man counts excellent is an offense to Him, but to value, esteem, or think highly of that which is of esteem with me, this is pleasing to me and such an opinion is excellent in my sight. What says Christ? "[My Father] loveth you, because ye have loved me" (John 16:27). Whoever has a high esteem for Christ, the Father has a high esteem for them. So it is said, "He that hath the Son, hath the Father"; the Father will be his and will do for him as a Father who receives and sets an honorable esteem on His Son.

But none will—none can—do this, except the brokenhearted, because they and they only are sensible of the want and worth of an interest in Him.

I dare appeal to all the world as to the truth of this and do say again that these and none but these have hearts of esteem in the sight of God. Alas! "The heart of the wicked is little worth" (Prov. 10:20), for it is destitute of a precious esteem of Christ and cannot be anything but destitute because it is not wounded, broken, and made sensible of the want of mercy by Him.

17

The Questioning Soul

Truly, says the soul, I think that by what you have said, I may have this blessed Jesus to be my advocate, for I truly think that I have entertained Him to be my advocate. I have also revealed my cause unto Him, committed both it and myself unto Him, and, as you say, I wait. Oh! I wait! And my eyes fail with looking upward. I wish I could hear how my soul stands in the sight of God and whether my sins, which I have committed since light and grace were given unto me, be, by my advocate, taken out of the hand of the Devil, and be, by my advocate, removed as far from me as the ends of the earth are separated. I wish I would hear whether the verdict has gone on my side, and what a shout there was among the angels when they saw it went well with me! But alas! I have waited, and that a long time, and have, as you advise, run from ordinance to minister and from minister to ordinance, or, as you phrase it, from the post to the carrier and from the carrier to the post house, to see if I could hear anything from heaven concerning how matters went about my soul there. I have also asked those who pass by the way if they saw Him whom my soul loves [Song 3:3], and if they had anything to communicate to me?

From *The Work of Jesus Christ as an Advocate*, in *Works*, 1:175.

But nothing can I get or find but general information, such as that I have an advocate there, that He pleads the cause of His people, and that He will thoroughly plead their cause. But what He has done for *me*, of that as yet I am ignorant. I doubt if my soul will by Him be effectually secured, that yet a conditional verdict will be awarded concerning me, that much bitter will be mixed with my sweet, and that I must drink gall and wormwood for my folly. For if David and Asa and Hezekiah and such good men were so served for their sins (2 Chron. 16:7, 12), why should I look for other dealing at the hand of God? But as to this, I will endeavor to "bear the indignation of the LORD, because I have sinned against him" (Mic. 7:9) and will count it an infinite mercy if this judgment comes to me from Him, that I may "not be condemned with the world" (1 Cor. 11:32). I know it is dreadful walking in darkness, but if that also will be the Lord's lot upon me, I pray that I may have faith enough to stay faithful to Him till death, when the clouds will blow over and I will see Him in the light of the living.

My enemy, the Devil, as you see, is of an enticing temper, and though he has accused me before the judgment seat of God, yet when he comes to me at any time, he wheedles and flatters as if he never did mean me harm. And I think he might get further advantage against me. However, I carry this belief now at a greater distance than I used to; and oh that I was at the remotest distance, not only from him but also from that self of mine that labors with him for my undoing!

But although I say these things now and to you, yet I have my solitary hours when I have other strange thoughts, for thus I think: My cause is bad, I have sinned, and I have been vile. I am ashamed of my own doings and have given my enemy the best end of the staff. The law and reason and my conscience plead for him against me, and all is true; he puts into his charge against me that I have sinned more times than there be hairs on my head. I know not anything that ever I did in my life but it had flaw or wrinkle or spot or some such thing in it. My eyes have seen vileness in the best of my doings. What then, think you, must God see in them? Nor can I do anything yet, for all I know that I am accused by my enemy before the judgment seat of God, better than what already is imperfect. "[I] lie down in [my] shame, and [my] confusion covereth [my face]"; "I have sinned, what shall I do unto thee, O thou preserver of men?" (Job 7:20; Jer. 3:25).

Reply
Well, soul, I have heard what you have said, and if all of it is true, it is good and gives me ground of hope that Jesus Christ has become your advocate. And if that be so, there is no doubt that your trial will come to a good conclusion. And do not be afraid because of the holiness of God, for your advocate has this for His advantage: He pleads before a judge who is just and against an enemy that is unholy and rejected. Nor let the thoughts of the badness of your cause terrify you too much. You have cause indeed to be humble, and you do well to cover your face with shame. And it is no matter how base and vile you

are in your own eyes, provided that it comes not by renewed acts of rebellion, but through a spiritual sight of your imperfections. Only let me advise you to stop here. Let neither your shame nor your self-abasing apprehension of yourself drive you from the firm and permanent ground of hope, which is the promise and the doctrine of an advocate with the Father. No, do not let the apprehension of the badness of your cause do it. For as much as He has never taken up a cause that was good, perfectly good, of itself—and His excellency is that He makes a man to stand who has a bad cause—He can make a bad cause good in a way of justice and righteousness.

Elstow Abbey Church

Bunyan was christened in this church building on November 30, 1628. Today, two stained glass windows portray scenes from *Pilgrim's Progress* and *The Holy War*.

18

A Contrite Heart before God

Reader, be advised, and consider…these things seriously, and compare your soul with them and with whatever else you find here that is written for your conviction and instruction.

If a broken heart and a contrite spirit is of such esteem with God, then this should encourage you to have it…and come to God with it. I know the great encouragement for men to come to God is that there "is one mediator between God and men, the man Christ Jesus" (1 Tim. 2:5). This, I say, is the great encouragement, and in its place there is none but that. But there are other encouragements subordinate to that, and a broken and a contrite spirit is one of them—this is evident in several places in Scripture.

So, you who carry a broken heart and a sorrowful spirit with you, when you go to God, tell Him your heart is wounded within you, that you have sorrow in your heart, and that you are sorry for your sins. But take heed of lying…. Confess also your sins unto Him, and tell Him they are continually before you. David made an argument of these things when he went to God by prayer. "O Lord," says he, "rebuke me not in thy wrath: neither chasten me in thy hot displeasure." But why so? "O!" says he, "Thine

---

From *The Acceptable Sacrifice*, in *Works*, 1:716–17.

A Contrite Heart before God

arrows stick fast in me, and thy hand presseth me sore. There is no soundness in my flesh, because of thine anger: neither is there any rest in my bones, because of my sin. For mine iniquities are gone over mine head: as a heavy burden they are too heavy for me. My wounds stink, and are corrupt, because of my foolishness. I am troubled; I am bowed down greatly; I go mourning all the day long. For my loins are filled with a loathsome disease: and there is no soundness in my flesh. I am feeble and sore broken; I have roared by reason of the disquietness of my heart. LORD, all my desire is before thee; and my groaning is not hid from thee. My heart panteth, my strength faileth me: as for the light of mine eyes, it also is gone from me. My lovers and my friends stand aloof from my sore," and so he goes on (Ps. 38:1–11).

These are the words, sighs, complaints, prayers, and arguments of a broken heart to God for mercy; and so are they, "Have mercy upon me, O God, according to thy loving-kindness; according unto the multitude of thy tender mercies blot out my transgressions. Wash me thoroughly from mine iniquity, and cleanse me from my sin. For I acknowledge my transgressions; and my sin is ever before me" (Ps. 51:1–3).

God allows poor creatures that can, without lying, thus to plead and argue with Him. "I am poor and sorrowful," said the good man to him, "Let thy salvation, O God, set me up on high" (Ps. 69:29). So, you who have a broken heart, take courage, God bids you to take courage. Say therefore to your soul, "Why art thou cast down, O my soul?" as usually the brokenhearted are. "And why art thou disquieted within me? Hope thou in God"; "I had fainted, unless I had believed...." Therefore "be of good courage, and he shall strengthen thine heart" (Pss. 42:11; 43:5; 27:13–14).

But alas! The brokenhearted are far off from this; they faint, they reckon themselves among the dead, and they think God will remember them no more. The thoughts of the greatness of God and His holiness and their own sins and vilenesses will certainly consume them. They feel guilt and anguish of soul, they go mourning all the day long, their mouth is full of gravel and gall, and they are made to drink draughts of wormwood and gall; so that he who believes must be an artist indeed who can come to God under his guilt and horror and plead in faith that the sacrifices of God are a broken heart, such as he had, and that "a broken and a contrite spirit God will not despise."

SECTION FOUR

True Humility

Bunyan's Wife before the Judge

Elizabeth Bunyan pled her husband's case before the House of Lords in London and then before Judge Hale at the assizes (sessions of the superior courts in English counties). When the judges asked her if her husband would be willing to leave preaching, she answered, "My lord, he dares not leave preaching, as long as he can speak."

19

Four Things That Are Acceptable to God

There are four things that are very acceptable to God. First is the sacrifice of the body of Christ for our sins. Of this you read in Hebrews 10, for there you have it preferred to all burnt offerings and sacrifices. It is this that pleases God; it is this that sanctified and so set the people acceptable in the sight of God.

Second, unfeigned love to God is counted better than all sacrifices or external parts of worship: "And to love [the Lord thy God] with all the heart, with all the understanding, and with all the soul, and with the strength, and to love his neighbor as himself, is more than all whole burnt offerings and sacrifices" (Mark 12:33).

Thirdly, to walk holily and humbly and obediently toward and before God is another (Mic. 6:8). "Hath the LORD as great a delight in burnt-offerings and sacrifices, as in obeying the voice of the LORD? Behold, to obey is better than to sacrifice, and to hearken, than the fat of rams" (1 Sam. 15:22).

Fourthly, and this is in our text: "The sacrifices of God are a broken spirit: a broken and a contrite heart, O God, thou wilt not despise" (Ps. 51:17).

From *The Acceptable Sacrifice*, in *Works*, 1:689.

20

The Evil Effects of the Sin of Pride

It is pride that makes a poor man so like the Devil in hell that he cannot in it be known to be the image and likeness of God. When the angels became devils, it was through their being lifted or puffed up with pride (1 Tim. 3:6). It is pride also that lifts or puffs up the heart of the sinner and so makes him bear the very image of the Devil.

Pride makes a man so odious in the sight of God that he will not, must not, come near His majesty. "Though the LORD be high, yet hath he respect unto the lowly; but the proud he knoweth afar off" (Ps. 138:6). Pride sets God and the soul at a distance; pride will not let a man come near God, nor will God let a proud man come near to Him. Now this is a dreadful thing.

Pride keeps God and the soul at a distance. "God resisteth the proud" (James 4:6). Resists, that is, He opposes him, He thrusts him from Him, He condemns his person and all his performances. The proud man may come to God's ordinances, but he may not come into His presence, have communion

From *The Life and Death of Mr. Badman: Presented to the World in a Familiar Dialogue between Mr. Wiseman and Mr. Attentive*, in *Works*, 3:645–46.

The Evil Effects of the Sin of Pride

with Him, or blessing from Him. For the high God resists him.

The Word says that "the LORD will destroy the house of the proud" (Prov. 15:25). He will destroy his house; it may be understood He will destroy him and his. In this way He destroyed proud Pharaoh, proud Korah, and many others.

Pride, where it comes and is entertained, is a certain forerunner of some judgment that is not far behind. When pride goes before, shame and destruction will follow after. "*When* pride cometh, then cometh shame" (Prov. 11:2). "Pride *goeth* before destruction, and a haughty spirit before a fall" (Prov. 16:18).

Persisting in pride makes the condition of a poor man as remediless as is that of the devils themselves (1 Tim. 3:6). And this, I fear, was Mr. Badman's condition and the reason that he died as he did, as I will presently show you.

But why should I talk of the particular actions, or rather the prodigious sins, of Mr. Badman, when his whole life and all his actions went, as it were, to the making up of one large body of sin? Instead of believing that there was a God, his mouth, his life, and his actions declared that he believed no such thing. His transgression "saith within my heart, that there [was] no fear of God before his eyes" (Ps. 36:1). Instead of honoring God and giving glory to Him for any of His mercies or any of His good providences toward him—for God is good to all and lets His sun shine and His rain fall upon the unthankful and unholy— he would ascribe glory to other causes. If they were mercies, he would ascribe them—if the open face of the providence did not give him opportunity to lie—to his own wit, labor, care, industry, cunning, or the like. If they were crosses, he would ascribe them to or count them as the offspring of fortune, ill luck, chance, the ill management of matters, the ill will of neighbors, or to his wife's being religious and spending, as he called it, too much time in reading, praying, or the like. It was not in his way to acknowledge God, that is, graciously, or His hand in things. But, as the prophet says, "Let favour be showed to the wicked, yet will he not learn righteousness" (Isa. 26:10). And again, "The people turneth not unto him that smiteth them, nor do they seek the LORD of hosts" (Isa. 9:13).... But farther, when by Providence he has been cast under the best means for his soul—for, as was showed before, he, having had a good master and before him a good father and after all a good wife, and being sometimes upon a journey and cast under the hearing of a good sermon, as he would sometimes for novelty's sake go to hear a good preacher—he was always without heart to make use of those means (Prov. 17:6)....

Instead of loving and honoring those who did bear on their foreheads the name and in their lives the image of Christ, they were his mocking song, the matter of his jests, and the objects of his slanders. He would either make a joke of their sober deportment, gracious language, quiet behavior, or else desperately swear that they did all in deceit and hypocrisy. He would endeavor to render godly men as odious and contemptible as he could; any lies that were made by any, to their disgrace, those he would avouch for truth and would not endure to be controlled. He

The Evil Effects of the Sin of Pride 137

was much like those that the prophet speaks of who would sit and slander his mother's son (Ps. 50:19–20). He would speak reproachfully of his wife, though his conscience told him and many would testify that she was a very virtuous woman. He would also raise slanders of his wife's friends himself, affirming that their doctrine tended to lasciviousness and that in their assemblies they acted like unsuitable men and women, that they committed uncleanness, and more. He was much like those who affirmed the apostle should say, "Let us do evil, that good may come" (Rom. 3:8). Or like those of whom it is written: "Report, say they, and we will report it" (Jer. 20:10). And if he could get anything by the end that had scandal in it, if it did but touch professors,[1] however falsely reported—oh! then he would glory, laugh, and be glad, and lay it upon the whole party.

---

1. *professors*: Christians, those who profess faith

21

Some Signs of a Broken Heart, of a Broken and Contrite Spirit

1. A brokenhearted man, such as is intended in the text, is a sensible man: He is brought to the exercise of all the senses of his soul. All others are dead, senseless, and without true feeling of what the brokenhearted man is sensible of....

2. He is a very sorrowful man. It is natural to one who is in pain and has his bones broken to be a grieved and sorrowful man. He is not of the jolly ones of the times, nor can be, for his bones and his heart are broken....

3. The man with a broken heart is a very humble man, for true humility is a sign of a broken heart. Hence, brokenness of heart, contrition of spirit, and humbleness of mind are put together. "To revive the spirit of the humble, and to revive the heart of the contrite ones" (Isa. 57:15)....

4. The brokenhearted man is a man who sees himself to be poor in spiritual things. Therefore as *humble* and *contrite* go together, so *poor* and *contrite* are put together in the Word: "But

to this man will I look, even to him that is *poor* and of a *contrite* spirit" (Isa. 66:2)....

5. Another sign of a broken heart is a crying, a crying out. Pain, you know, will make one cry; go to them who have upon them the anguish of broken bones and see if they do not cry. Anguish makes them cry. This is that which quickly follows, if once your heart is broken and your spirit indeed made contrite....

6. Another sign of a broken heart, and of a contrite spirit, is that it trembles at God's Word. "To him that is poor, and of a contrite spirit, and trembleth at my word" (Isa. 6:2).

SECTION FIVE

Christian Ethics

The Life and Death of Mr. Badman

This illustration from an early edition shows an informant spying on dissenters during an unauthorized gathering so that he can report them to the authorities.

22

A Simple Christian's View of Extortion

We have a great many people in the country who live all their days in the practice and under the guilt of extortion. Alas! People that think scorn to be so accounted. For example, there is a poor body that dwells, we will suppose, so many miles from the market, and this man wants a bushel of grist, a pound of butter, or a cheese for himself, his wife, and poor children. But dwelling so far from the market means that if he goes there, he will lose a day's work, which will be eightpence or tenpence damage to him, and that is something to a poor man.

So he goes to one of his masters or dames for what he wants and asks them to help him with such a thing. "Yes," they say, "you may have it," but they will...perhaps make him pay as much or more for it at home as they can get when they have carried it five miles to a market, and that too for the refuse of their commodity. But in this the women are especially faulty in the sale of their butter and cheese. Now this is a kind of extortion; it is making a prey of the necessity of the poor; it is a grinding of their faces, a buying and selling of them.

From *The Life and Death of Mr. Badman*, in *Works*, 3:637–38.

But above all, your hucksters who buy up the poor man's food by wholesale and sell it to him again for unreasonable gains by retail and, as we call it, by piecemeal, they are got into a way, after a stinging rate, to play their game upon such by extortion. I mean such who buy up butter, cheese, eggs, and bacon by wholesale and sell it again, as they call it, by pennyworths, two pennyworths, a halfpennyworth, or the like, to the poor all the week after the market is past.

These, though I will not condemn them all, do, many of them, bite and pinch the poor by this kind of evil dealing. These destroy the poor because he is poor, and that is a grievous sin. "He that oppresseth the poor to increase his riches, and he that giveth to the rich, shall surely come to want" (Prov. 22:16). He says again, "Rob not the poor because he is poor, neither oppress the afflicted in the gate: for the LORD will plead their cause, and spoil the soul of those that spoiled them" (Prov. 22:22–23).

Oh that he who pinches and grinds the face of the poor would take notice of these two Scriptures! Here is threatened the destruction of the estate and of the soul too of those who oppress the poor. Their soul we will see better where and in what condition that is in when the day of doom is come, but for the estates of such, they usually quickly molder; and that sometimes all men, and sometimes no man knows how.

Besides, these are usurers—they take usury for sustenance—a practice that the Lord has forbidden (Deut. 23:19). And because they cannot do it so well on the market day, they do it, as I said, when the market is over. For then the poor fall into their

A Simple Christian's View of Extortion 145

mouths and are necessitated to have, as they can, for their need, and they are resolved they will have to pay soundly for it. Perhaps some will find fault for my meddling in this way with other folks' matters and for my prying into the secrets of their iniquity. But to such I would say that since such actions are evil, it is time they were hissed out of the world. For all who do such things offend God, wrong their neighbor, and, like Mr. Badman, provoke God to judgment.

23

Instructions for Righteous Trading

This question is thought to be frivolous by all that are of Mr. Badman's way; it is also difficult in itself, yet I will endeavor to shape you an answer. First to the matter of the question of...how a tradesman should, in trading, keep a good conscience, and a buyer or seller as well. Secondly, how he should prepare himself for this work and live in the practice of it. For the first, he must observe what has been said before; to wit, he must have conscience to God, charity to his neighbor, and, I will add, much moderation in dealing. Let him therefore keep within the bounds of the affirmative of those...reasons...to prove that men should only, in their dealing, do justly and mercifully between man and man, and then there will be no great fear of wronging the seller, buyer, or himself. But particularly to prepare or instruct a man to this work, [consider the following]:...

Consider that the getting of wealth dishonestly—as he does who gets it without good conscience and charity to his neighbor—is a great offender against God. Because of this God says, "I have smitten mine hand at thy dishonest gain which thou hast made"

From *The Life and Death of Mr. Badman*, in *Works*, 3:640–42.

(Ezek. 22:13). It is a manner of speech that shows anger in the very making mention of the crime.

Consider also that a little, honestly gotten, though it may yield you with only a dinner of herbs at a time, will yield more peace than will a stalled ox obtained by dishonest means (Prov. 15:17). "Better is a little with righteousness, than great revenues without right" (Prov. 16:8; 1 Sam. 2:5)....

Be sure that you remember that you know not the day of your death. Remember also that when death comes, God will give possessions for which you have labored and for which perhaps you endangered your soul to someone else, and you don't know who that will be, whether he will be a wise man or a fool. And then, "what profit hath he that hath laboured for the wind?" (Eccl. 5:16).

Besides, you will have nothing that you may so much as carry away in your hand at death. Guilt shall go with you if you have gotten your substance dishonestly, and the one you leave it to will receive it to his harm. These things duly considered and made use of by you in preparing your heart for the calling of buying and selling, I come, in the next place, to show you how you should live in the practical part of this art. Should you buy or sell?

If you sell, do not commend; if you buy, do not dispraise; only act in such a way as to give each item its just value and worth. For you cannot do otherwise, knowingly, unless you have a covetous and wicked mind. This is why commodities are overvalued by the seller and also undervalued by the buyer. "It is naught, it is naught, saith the buyer, but when he hath got his bargain he boasteth thereof" (Prov. 20:14). What has this man done now but lied in the dispraising of his bargain? And why did he dispraise it, but of a covetous mind to wrong and beguile the seller?

Are you a seller, and do things grow dear? Set not your hand to help or hold them up higher; this cannot be done without wickedness either, for this is a making of the shekel great (Amos 8:5). Are you a buyer, and do things grow dear? Use no cunning or deceitful language to pull them down, for that can only be done wickedly too. What then should we do, will you say? Why I answer, leave things to the providence of God, and with moderation submit to His hand. But since, when they are growing dear, the hand that upholds the price is, for the time, more strong than that which would pull it down—that being the hand of the seller, who loves to have it dear, especially if it should rise in his hand. Therefore I say, take heed not to cause harm to yourself and your neighbor, and do not have a hand in unrighteous trading in this way:

By crying out scarcity, scarcity, beyond the truth and state of things; especially take heed of doing of this by way of a prognostic for time to come. It was for this for which the king was trodden to death in the gate of Samaria, which you read of in the second book of Kings (2 Kings 7:17). This sin has a double evil in it: (1) It belies the present blessing of God among us; and (2) it undervalues the riches of His goodness, which can make all good things abound toward us.

This wicked thing may be done by hoarding up when the hunger and necessity of the poor call for it. Now, that God may show His dislike against this, He does, as it were, license the people to curse such

Instructions for Righteous Trading

a hoarder—"He that withholdeth corn, the people shall curse him, but blessing shall be upon the head of him that selleth it" (Prov. 11:26).

But if things will rise, be grieved and be also moderate in all your selling. Be sure to let the poor have a pennyworth, and sell your corn to those in need. When you show mercy to the poor in your selling to him, for his sake, because he is poor, undersell the market. This is to buy and sell with good conscience: You do not wrong your buyer; you do not wrong your conscience; and you do not wrong yourself, for God will surely repay you (Isa. 57:6–8). I have spoken concerning corn, but your duty is to "let your moderation [in all things] be known unto all men. The Lord is at hand" (Phil. 4:5).

24

Strictures against Fraudulent Bankruptcy

The Word of God forbids this wickedness, and to make it more odious in our eyes, it joins it with theft and robbery. "Thou shalt not," says God, "defraud thy neighbour, neither rob him" (Lev. 19:13). "Thou shalt not defraud," that is, deceive or beguile. Now thus to break is to defraud, deceive, and beguile, which is, as you see, forbidden by the God of heaven: "Thou shalt not defraud thy neighbour, neither rob him." It is a kind of theft and robbery to defraud and beguile. It is a vile robbing of his shop and picking of his pocket, a thing odious to reason and conscience and contrary to the law of nature. *It is a designed piece of wickedness, and therefore a double sin* (emphasis added). A man cannot do this great wickedness suddenly, through a violent assault of Satan. He who will commit this sin must have time to deliberate, that by invention he may make it formidable, using lies and high dissimulations. He who commits this wickedness must first hatch it upon his bed, beat

---

From *The Life and Death of Mr. Badman*, in *Works*, 3:629–31. The editor's footnote 1 (628) states: "Fraudulent bankruptcy is a sore and prevailing evil. It is thieving under the protection of the law. How many live in state, until their creditors give a few shillings in the pound, and the bankrupt gets the curse of God upon his soul!"

his head about it, and lay his plot strong so that to the completing of such a wickedness, there must be adjoined many sins, and they too must go hand in hand until it is completed. But what does the Scripture say? "[Let] no man go beyond and defraud his brother in any matter: because that the Lord is the avenger of all such" (1 Thess. 4:6).

The apostle testifies again, where he says, "But he that doeth wrong, shall receive for the wrong which he hath done; and there is no respect of persons" (Col. 3:25).... There is no man, be he what he will, if he will be guilty of this sin—of going beyond, of beguiling of, and doing wrong to his brother— whom God will not call to an account for what he has done and will pay him with vengeance for it too; for "there is no respect of persons."

I might add that this sin of wronging, of going beyond and defrauding of my neighbor, is like that first prank that the Devil played with our first parents, as the altar that Urijah built for Ahaz was taken from the fashion of that that stood at Damascus, to be the very pattern of it. "The serpent beguiled me," says Eve; Mr. Badman beguiles his creditors. The serpent beguiled Eve with lying promises of gain, and so did he beguile his creditors. The serpent said one thing and meant another when he beguiled Eve, and so did Mr. Badman when he beguiled his creditors....

Secondly...let this man consider how and by what means he was brought into such a condition that he could not pay his just debts, to wit, whether it was by his own remissness in his calling, by living too high in diet or apparel, by lending too lavishly that which was none of his own, to his loss, or whether it was by the immediate hand and judgment of God.

If by searching he finds that this has come upon him through remissness in his calling, extravagancies in his family, or the like, let him labor for a sense of his sin and wickedness—for he has sinned against the Lord. First, there is...his being slothful in business and in not providing, to wit, of his own, by the sweat of his brow or other honest ways, for those of his own house (Rom. 12:11; 1 Tim. 5:8). And secondly, in being lavish in diet and apparel in the family, or in lending to others that which was not his own. This cannot be done with good conscience. It is both against reason and nature, and therefore must be a sin against God.... To be slothful and a waster too is to be, as it were, a double sinner....

Thirdly...let that man again consider this with himself: "Perhaps God is now changing my condition and state in the world. He has let me live in fashion, in fullness, and abundance of worldly glory, and I did not to His glory improve, as I should have, His good dispensation to me. But when I lived in full and fat pasture, I did there lift up the heel (Deut. 32:15). Therefore, He will now turn me to hard times, that with leanness and hunger and meanness and want, I may spend the rest of my days." But let him do this without murmuring and repining; let him do it in a godly manner, submitting himself to the judgment of God. "[Let] the rich [rejoice] in that he is made low" (James 1:10).

This is duty, and it may be privilege to those who are under this hand of God. And for your

Strictures against Fraudulent Bankruptcy 153

encouragement to this hard work—for this is a hard work—consider these four things:

1. This is right submission under God's hand and the way to be exalted in God's time. When God would have Job embrace the dunghill, he embraces it and says, "The LORD gave, and the LORD hath taken away, blessed be the name of the LORD" (Job 1:21).

2. Consider that there are also blessings, more than all the world is aware of, that attend a low condition. A poor condition does have preventing mercy along with it. The poor, because they are poor, are not capable of sinning against God as the rich man does (Ps. 49:6).

3. The poor man can more clearly see himself preserved by the providence of God than the rich, for the rich man trusts in the abundance of his riches.

4. It may be that God has made you poor because He wants to make you rich. "Hearken, my beloved brethren, Hath not God chosen the poor of this world, rich in faith, and heirs of the kingdom which God hath promised to them that love him?" (James 2:5).

SECTION SIX

The Gospel Applied

Fac Simile of the Will of John Bunyan.

Facsimile of Bunyan's Will

25

What It Is to Be Offered

By saying he was "to be offered," Paul alludes to some of the sacrifices that of old were under the law and thereby signifies to Timothy that his death and martyrdom for the gospel should be both sweet in the nostrils of God and of great profit to His church in this world; for so were the sacrifices of old. Paul, therefore, lifts his eyes up higher than simply to look upon death, as it is the common fate of men; and he had good reason to do it, for his death was violent. It was also for Christ and for His church and truth; and it is usual with Paul thus to set out the suffering of the saints, which they undergo for the name and testimony of Jesus. Paul says our prayers are a sacrifice; our praises, thanksgiving, and mortification are sacrifices; acts of charity and the offering up of the Gentiles are sacrifices sanctified by the Holy Ghost; and here, his death also must be for a sacrifice and an acceptable offering to God (Heb. 13:15–16; Rom. 12:1–2; 15:16).

Peter also says we are priests who offer up "spiritual sacrifices, acceptable to God by Jesus Christ" (1 Peter 2:5). It seems to Paul that the death of a Christian for Jesus' sake must be counted as one of

From "Paul's Departure and Crown, or An Exposition Upon 2 Timothy 4:6–8," in *Works*, 1:724–25.

these sacrifices. Besides, Paul further insinuates this by some other sentences in his epistles, as by that in the Epistle to the Colossians, where he says, "[I] now rejoice in my sufferings for you, and fill up that which is behind of the afflictions of Christ in my flesh for his body's sake, which is the church" (Col. 1:24). Not by way of merit, for so Christ alone, and that by once being offered Himself, hath perfected forever them that are sanctified (see Heb. 10:10–14). But his meaning is that as Christ was offered in sacrifice for His church as a savior, so Paul would offer himself as a sacrifice for Christ's church, as a saint, as a minister, and as one who was counted faithful. "Yea," he says, "and if I be offered upon the sacrifice and service of your faith, I joy, and rejoice with you all" (Phil. 2:17).

The sufferings of the saints are of a redeeming virtue.... By their patient enduring and losing their blood for the Word, they recover the truths of God that have been buried in anti-Christian rubbish, truths hidden under that soil and slur that have clung onto them for a long time. And it is said that they overcame him, the beast, "by the blood of the Lamb, and by the word of their testimony, and they loved not their lives unto the death" (Rev. 12:11). They overcame him; that is, they recovered the truth from under his aspersions, and delivered it from all its enemies. David says, "The words of the LORD are... as silver tried in a furnace of earth, purified seven times" (Ps. 12:6). What is this furnace of earth but the body of the saints of God in which the Word is tried as by fire in persecution, even "purified seven times," that is, brought forth at last by the death of the Christians in its purity before the world.

What It Is to Be Offered

Learn thus much:

Learn that the judgment that is made of our sufferings by carnal men is nothing at all to be heeded; they do not see the glory that is wrapped up in our cause, nor the innocence and goodness of our conscience in our enduring of these afflictions. They judge according to the flesh, according to outward appearance. For so, indeed, we seem to lie under contempt and to be in a disgraceful condition, but all things here are converted to another use and end.

We learn also from this the reason why some in days before us have made light of the rage of the world; instead they have laughed at destruction when it comes (Job 5:21–22). They have gone forth to meet the armed men, and with Job's war horse, "mocketh at fear, and is not affrighted, neither turneth he back from the sword. The quiver rattleth against him, the glittering spear and the shield...he saith among the trumpets" (Job 39:22–25).... As Paul...says, "Therefore I take pleasure in infirmities, in reproaches, in necessities, in persecutions, in distresses, for Christ's sake" (2 Cor. 12:10).

Learn also in this to be confident so that your sufferings have their sound and a voice before God and men. First, before God, to provoke Him to vengeance, "when he maketh inquisition for blood" (Ps. 9:12; Gen. 4:9–11). The blood of Abel cried until it brought down wrath upon Cain; and so did the blood of Christ and His apostles, till it had laid Jerusalem upon heaps. Secondly, your blood will also have a voice before men, and that possibly for their good. The faithful Christian, in his patient suffering, knows not what work he may do for God. Who knows but your blood may be so remembered by your children, neighbors, and enemies as to convince them you were for the truth? Who knows that their thoughts of your resolution for Christ in your resisting unto blood may have so good an effect upon some as to persuade them to unite with His ways? The three children in the fiery furnace made Nebuchadnezzar cry out that there was no God like theirs! Indeed, this is hard labor, but be content: The dearer you pay for it to win the souls of others, the greater will be your crown when the Lord, the righteous Judge, does appear. And in the meanwhile, your death will be as a sacrifice pleasing to God and His saints.

The Bunyan Oak

An early twentieth-century photograph of the "natural pulpit" Bunyan would use for open-air services in the fields near Bedford. In 1660, Bunyan was arrested at a farmhouse about a half-mile from this spot.

26

Prison Meditations

1. Friend, I salute you in the Lord,
    And wish you may abound
   In faith, and have a good regard
    To keep on holy ground.

2. You do encourage me to hold
    My head above the flood,
   Your counsel better is than gold,
    In need thereof I stood.

3. Good counsel's good at any time,
    The wise will it receive,
   Though fools count he commits a crime
    Who does good counsel give.

4. I take it kindly at your hand
    You did unto me write,
   My feet upon Mount Zion stand,
    In that take your delight.

From "Prison Meditations, Directed to the Heart of Suffering Saints and Reigning Sinners," in *Works*, 1:*63–*66. Bunyan wrote seventy stanzas from prison in 1665 and later published them after his initial twelve-year incarceration. He demonstrates the harshness of confinement and the sweetness found in communion with Christ. These meditations provide a wonderful solace to those walking through suffering.

5. I am, indeed, in prison now
    In body, but my mind
  Is free to study Christ, and how
    Unto me He is kind.

6. For though men keep my outward man
    Within their locks and bars,
  Yet by the faith of Christ I can
    Mount higher than the stars.

7. Their fetters cannot spirits tame,
    Nor tie up God from me;
  My faith and hope they cannot lame,
    Above them I will be.

8. I here am very much refreshed
    To think when I was out,
  I preached life and peace and rest
    To sinners round about.

9. My business then was souls to save,
    By preaching grace and faith;
  Of which the comfort now I have,
    And have it shall till death.

10. They were no fables that I taught,
    Devised by cunning men,
  But God's own Word, by which were caught
    Some sinners now and then.

11. Whose souls by it were made to see
    The evil of their sin;
  And need of Christ to make them free
    From death which they were in.

12. And now those very hearts that then
	Were foes unto the Lord,
    Embrace His Christ and truth like men
    	Conquered by His Word.

13. I hear them sigh and groan and cry
    	For grace to God above;
    They loathe their sin, and to it die,
    	'Tis holiness they love.

14. This was the work I was about
    	When hands on me they laid,
    'Twas this from which they plucked me out,
    	And vilely to me said,

15. You heretic, deceiver, come,
    	To prison you must go;
    You preach abroad, and keep not home,
    	You are the church's foe.

16. But having peace within my soul,
    	And truth on every side,
    I could with comfort them control,
    	And at their charge deride.

17. Wherefore to prison they me sent,
    	Where to this day I lie,
    And can with very much content
    	For my profession die.

18. The prison very sweet to me
    	Has been since I came here,
    And so would also hanging be,
    	If God would there appear.

19. Here dwells good conscience, also peace
    Here be my garments white;
    Here, though in bonds, I have release
    From guilt, which else would bite.

20. When they do talk of banishment,
    Of death, or such-like things;
    Then to me God sends heart's content,
    That like a fountain springs.

21. Alas! They little think what peace
    They help me to, for by
    Their rage my comforts do increase;
    Bless God therefore do I.

22. If they do give me gall to drink,
    Then God does sweetening cast
    So much thereto, that they can't think
    How bravely it does taste.

23. For, as the Devil sets before
    Me heaviness and grief,
    So God sets Christ and grace much more,
    Whereby I take relief.

....

27. God sometimes visits prisons more
    Than lordly palaces,
    He often knocks at our door,
    When He their houses miss.

28. The truth and life of heavenly things
    Lift up our hearts on high,
    And carry us on eagles' wings,
    Beyond carnality.

29. It takes away those clogs that hold
    The hearts of other men,
And makes us lively, strong and bold
    Thus to oppose their sin.

....

34. This goal to us is as a hill,
    From whence we plainly see
Beyond this world, and take our fill
    Of things that lasting be.

35. From hence we see the emptiness
    Of all this world contains;
And here we feel the blessedness
    That for us yet remains.

36. Here we can see how all men play
    Their parts, as on a stage,
How good men suffer for God's way,
    And bad men at them rage.

....

48. Again, we see what glory 'tis
    Freely to bear our cross
For Him who for us took up His,
    When He our servant was.

....

50. Just thus it is we suffer here
    For Him a little pain,
Who, when He does again appear,
    Will with Him let us reign.

....

Prison Meditations

59. Know then, true valor there does dwell
    Where men engage for God,
    Against the Devil, death, and hell,
    And bear the wicked's rod.

60. These be the men that God does count
    Of high and noble mind;
    These be the men that do surmount
    What you in nature find.

....

69. And what though they us dear do cost,
    Yet let us buy them so;
    We shall not count our labor lost
    When we see others' woe.

70. And let saints be no longer blamed
    By carnal policy;
    But let the wicked be asham'd
    Of their malignity.

SECTION SEVEN

Warnings

Bunyan Dreaming

Bunyan's famous opening sentence of *Pilgrim's Progress* suggests that the story is a dream: "As I walked through the wilderness of this world, I lighted on a certain place where was a den, and laid me down…to sleep; and…I dreamed a dream."

27

God Would Show the Greatness of His Anger against Sin and Sinners

Therefore, when God would show the greatness of His anger against sin and sinners in one word, He says they are "joined to idols; let [them] alone" (Hos. 4:17). Let them alone, that is, do not disturb them; let them go on without control; let the Devil enjoy them peaceably; let him carry them out of the world, unconverted, quietly. This is one of the sorest of judgments and bespeaks the burning anger of God against sinful men. See also when you come home, the fourteenth verse of the fourth chapter of Hosea: "I will not punish your daughters when they commit whoredom." He will let them alone; they will live and die in their sins.

My…argument is drawn from that saying of Christ: "He hath blinded their eyes, and hardened their heart; that they should not see with their eyes, nor understand with their heart, and be converted, and I should heal them" (John 12:40). There are three things that I will take notice of from these words.

There can be no conversion to God where the eye is darkened and the heart hardened. The eye must

---

From *The Life and Death of Mr. Badman*, in *Works*, 3:662–63.

first be made to see and the heart to break and relent under and for sin or else there can be no conversion. "He hath blinded their eyes, and hardened their heart, lest they should see, and understand and" so "be converted." And this was clearly Mr. Badman's case; he lived a wicked life and also died with his eyes shut and heart hardened, as is manifest in that a sinful life was joined with a quiet death. And all for that he should not be converted, but partake of the fruit of his sinful life in hellfire.

The second thing that I take notice of from these words is that this is a dispensation and manifestation of God's anger against a man for his sin. When God is angry with men—I mean, when He is so angry with them—this among many is one of the judgments that He gives them up unto, to wit, to blindness of mind and hardness of heart, which He also suffers to accompany them till they enter the gates of death. And then and there and not short of then and there, their eyes come to be opened. Hence it is said of the rich man mentioned in Luke: He died, and in hell he lifted up his eyes (see Luke 16:22–23). This implies that he did not lift them up before; he neither saw what he had done, nor whither he was going till he came to the place of execution, even into hell. He died asleep in his soul; he died besotted, stupefied, and so consequently for quietness like a child or lamb, even as Mr. Badman did. This was a sign of God's anger; He had a mind to damn him for his sins and therefore would not let him see nor have a heart to repent for them, in case he is converted and his damnation, which God had appointed, be frustrated. "Lest they should be converted, and I should heal them."

The third thing...is that a sinful life and a quiet death annexed to it is the ready, the open, the beaten, the common highway to hell. There is no surer sign of damnation than for a man to die quietly after a sinful life. I do not say that all wicked men who are molested at their death with a sense of sin and fears of hell do therefore go to heaven, for some are also made to see and are left to despair, not converted by seeing, that they might go roaring out of this world to their place. But I say there is no surer sign of a man's damnation than to die quietly after a sinful life; than to sin and die with his eyes shut; than to sin and die with a heart that cannot repent. "He hath blinded their eyes and hardened their heart, that they should not see with their eyes, nor understand with their heart" (John 12:40). No, not so long as they are in this world, "lest they should see with their eyes...and understand with their heart, and should be converted, and I should heal them" (Acts 28:26–27; Rom. 2:1–5).

God has a judgment for wicked men; God will be even with wicked men. God knows how to reserve the ungodly for the day of judgment to be punished (2 Peter 2). And this is one of His ways by which He does it. Thus it was with Mr. Badman.

It is said in the book of Psalms concerning the wicked: "There are no bands in their death, but their strength is firm" (Ps. 73:4). By "no bands" he means no troubles, no gracious chastisements, no such corrections for sin as God's people receive for theirs, which many times they receive at the time of their death. Therefore, He adds concerning the wicked: "They are not in trouble then as other men, neither are they plagued like other men" (Ps. 73:5); but go as securely out of the world as if they had never sinned against God and put their own souls into danger of damnation. "There are no bands in their death."

So you will hear these men boast of their faith and hope in God's mercy when they lie upon their deathbed; yes, you will hear them speak as confidently of their salvation as if they had served God all their days when the truth is, the bottom of this, their boasting, is because they have no bands in their death. Their sin and base life comes not into their mind to correct them and bring them to repentance; but presumptuous thoughts and a hope and faith of the Devil's making possess their soul to their own eternal undoing (Job 8:13–14).

28

Reasons or Causes for Pride

The first [cause for pride] is such persons are led by their own hearts rather than by the Word of God (Mark 7:21–23).... The original fountain of pride is the heart. For out of the heart comes pride; it is, therefore, because they are led by their hearts, which naturally tend to lift them up in pride. This pride of heart tempts them, and by its deceits overcomes them. It truly puts a bewitching virtue into their peacock's feathers, and then they are swallowed up with the vanity of them (Obad. 3).

Another reason professors are so proud—for those we are talking of now—is because they are more apt to take example from those who are of the world than they are to take example from those who are saints indeed. Pride is of the world. "For all that is in the world, the lust of the flesh, and the lust of the eyes, and the pride of life, is not of the Father, but is of the world" (1 John 2:16). Of the world, therefore, professors learn to be proud. But they should not take them for example. It will be objected, "No, nor your saints neither, for you are as proud as others"; well, let those who are guilty take shame. But when I say professors should take example for their life by those who are saints indeed, I mean, as Peter says, they

From *The Life and Death of Mr. Badman*, in *Works*, 3:644–45.

should take example of those "in old time" (1 Peter 3:5). For those "of old time" were the best; therefore to these he directed us for our pattern. Let the wives' conversation be chaste and also coupled with fear. "Whose adorning," Peter says, "let it not be that outward adorning of plaiting the hair, and of wearing of gold, or of putting on of apparel; but let it be the hidden man of the heart, in that which is not corruptible, even the ornament of a meek and quiet spirit, which is in the sight of God of great price. For after this manner, in the old time, the holy women also, who trusted in God, adorned themselves, being in subjection unto their own husbands" (1 Peter 3:3–5).

Another reason is because they have forgotten the pollution of their nature. For the remembrance of that keeps us humble, and…if we be kept humble, we will be at a distance from pride. The proud and the humble are set in opposition; "God resisteth the proud, but giveth grace unto the humble." And can it be imagined that a sensible Christian should be a proud one? Sense of baseness tends to lay us low, not to lift us up with pride—not with pride of heart or pride of life. But when a man begins to forget what he is, then he, if ever, begins to be proud. I think it is one of the most senseless and ridiculous things in the world that a man should be proud of that which is given him on purpose to cover the shame of his nakedness.

Persons who are proud have gotten God and His holiness out of their sight. If God was before them as He is behind their back, and if they saw Him in His holiness as He sees them in their sins and shame, they would take but little pleasure in their foolish skills. The holiness of God makes the angels cover their faces and crumbles Christians, when they behold it, into dust and ashes. And as His majesty is, such is His Word (Isa. 6). Therefore, those who come before His Word while tolerating their own pride abuse it.

Lastly, what can be the end of those who are proud in the decking of themselves after their antic manner? Why are they for going with their bull's foretops,[1] with their naked shoulders, and breasts hanging out like a cow's udder? Why are they for painting their faces, for stretching out their neck, and for putting themselves into all the formalities that proud fancy leads them to? Is it because they would honor God? Because they would adorn the gospel? Because they would beautify religion and make sinners to fall in love with their own salvation? No, no, it is rather to please their lusts, to satisfy their wild and extravagant fancies; and I wish none of it would stir up lust in others because they may commit uncleanness with them. I believe, whatever is their end, this is one of the great designs of the Devil, and I believe also that Satan has drawn more into the sin of uncleanness by the spangling show of fine clothes than he could possibly have drawn into it without them. I wonder what it was that of old was called the attire of a harlot; certainly it could not be more bewitching and tempting than are the garments of many professors this day.

---

1. *bull's foretop*: "A tuft of hair worn on a man's forehead, or a projecting conspicuous part of the women's caps worn by the fashionable of that time" (editor's footnote 1, *Life and Death of Mr. Badman*, in *Works*, 3:645).

29

Of the Unchangeableness of Eternal Reprobation

Many opinions have passed through the hearts of the sons of men concerning reprobation, most of them endeavoring to try to hold it forth in such a way as to, if not heal their conscience slightly, yet still maintain their own opinion and judgment of other things, wringing the Word this way and that…for their own purpose. They also want to frame within their soul such an imagination of God and His acts in eternity as would suit with such opinions, and so present this teaching to all the world. And they have with greatest labor strained unweariedly with this above many other truths, because of the grim and dreadful appearance it carries in most men's apprehensions. But none of these things, however they may please the creature, can, by any means in any measure, cause God to undo, unsay, or undetermine what He has decreed and established concerning this doctrine.

Because they are not in accord with His nature, especially in these foundation acts—"The founda-

From *Reprobation Asserted of the Doctrine of Eternal Election and Reprobation Promiscuously Handled, in Eleven Chapters, Wherein the Most Material Objections Made by the Opposers of This Doctrine, Are Fully Answered; Several Doubts Removed, and Sundry Cases of Conscience Resolved*, in *Works*, 2:341–42.

tion of God standeth sure" (2 Tim. 2:19)—even touching reprobation, "that the purpose of God according to election might stand" (Rom. 9:11). Solomon says, "I know that whatsoever God doeth, it shall be for ever: nothing can be put to it, nor any thing taken from it" (Eccl. 3:14). "Hath he said, and shall he not do it? Or hath he spoken, and shall he not make it good?" (Num. 23:19). His decrees are composed according to His eternal wisdom, established upon His unchangeable will, governed by His knowledge, prudence, power, justice, and mercy, and are brought to conclusion, on His part, in perfect holiness through the abiding of His most blessed truth and faithfulness: "He is the rock, his work is perfect: for all his ways are judgment: a God of truth and without iniquity, just and right is he" (Deut. 32:4).

This decree is made sure by the number, measure, and bounds of election, for election and reprobation do enclose all reasonable creatures—that is, either the one or the other. Election is for those who are set apart for glory, and reprobation is for those left out of this choice.

Now as touching the elect, they are by this decree confined to that limited number of persons that must amount to the complete making up the fullness of the mystical body of Christ. The elect are so confined by this eternal purpose that nothing can be diminished from or added to them, and so it is that they are called His body, and members in particular: "The fulness of him that filleth all in all" (Eph. 1:23) and "the measure of the stature of the fullness of Christ" (Eph. 4:13). That body, considering Him as the head, in conclusion makes up one perfect man and holy temple for the Lord. These are called Christ's substance, inheritance, and lot (Ps. 16) and are said to be booked, marked, and sealed with God's most excellent knowledge, approbation, and liking (2 Tim. 2:19). As Christ said to His Father, "Thine eyes did see my substance, yet being unperfect; and in thy book all my members were written, which in continuance were fashioned, when as yet there was none of them" (Ps. 139:16). This being as it is, I say, it is in the first place impossible that any of those members should be lost, for "who shall lay any thing to the charge of God's elect?" (Rom. 8:33). And because they are, as to number, in every way sufficient, being His body, and so by their completing to be made a perfect man, all others are rejected so that the "purpose of God according to election might stand" (Rom. 9:11). Besides, it would not only argue weakness in the decree but monstrousness in the body if, after this, any appointed should be lost, or any besides them be added to them (Matt. 24:24).

Further, that all may see how punctual, exact, and thorough this decree of election is, God has not only as to number and quantity confined the persons, but also determined and measured, and that before the world, the number of the gifts and graces that are to be bestowed on these members in general, and also what graces and gifts to be bestowed on this or that member in particular: He "hath blessed us with all spiritual blessings...in Christ, according as he hath chosen us in him before the foundation of the world" (Eph. 1:3–4). And He bestows them in time upon us, "according to the eternal purpose which he purposed in Christ Jesus our Lord" (Eph. 3:11). He has given to the eye the grace that belongs to the eye, and to the hand that which He also has appointed for it. And so to every other member of the body elect, He deals out to them their determined measure of grace and gifts most fit for their place and office. So the decree is established, both of the saved and also the nonelect (Rom. 12:3; Eph. 4:12–13, 16; Col. 2:19). But again, another thing that establishes this decree of eternal reprobation is the weakness that sin, in the Fall and since, has brought all reprobates into: For though it be most true that sin is no cause of eternal reprobation, yet seeing that sin has seized the reprobate, it means the decree must be the faster settled. If the king, for this or the other weighty reason, decrees not to give this or that man who yet did never offend him a place in his privy chamber, and then after this the man is infected with the plague, this rather fastens than loosens the king's decree. As the angels that were left out of God's election, by reason of the sin they committed after, are so far off from being by that received into God's decree, that they are therefore bound for it in chains of everlasting darkness to the judgment of the great day.

30

Warning to False Professors of Religion

Why, I would say that I hope no good man, no man of good conscience, no man who either fears God, regards the credit of religion, the peace of God's people, or the salvation of his own soul, will do thus.[1] Such professors, perhaps, there may be, and who upon earth can help it? There are jades of all colors. If men will profess and make their profession a stalking horse[2] to beguile their neighbors of their estates, as Mr. Badman himself did when he beguiled her that now is with sorrow his wife, who can help it? The churches of old were pestered with such, and therefore it is no marvel if these perilous difficult times be what they are. But mark how the apostle words it: "Nay, ye do wrong, and defraud, and that your brethren. Know ye not that the unrighteous shall not inherit the kingdom of God? Be not deceived, neither fornicators, nor idolators, nor adulterers, nor effeminate, nor abusers of themselves with mankind, nor thieves, nor covetous, nor drunkards,

---

From *The Life and Death of Mr. Badman*, in *Works*, 632–33.

1. "Do thus" in this context means to "beguile men, debauch their consciences, [and] sin against their profession."

2. *stalking horse*: a horse or a figure like a horse behind which a hunter stalks game

nor revilers, nor extortioners, shall inherit the kingdom of God" (1 Cor. 6:8–10; see also 2 Tim. 3:1–5).

None of these will be saved in this state, nor will profession deliver them from the censure of the godly when it becomes apparent what they are. But their profession we cannot help. How can we help it if men should ascribe to themselves the title of holy ones, godly ones, zealous ones, self-denying ones, or any other such glorious title? And while they call themselves these things, they are truly rogues for all evil, sin, and villainy imaginable—who could help it? True, they are a scandal to religion, a grief to the honest-hearted, an offense to the world, and a stumbling stone to the weak, and these offenses have come, do come, and will come, do what all the world can; but woe to them through whom they come (Matt. 18:6–8). Let such professors therefore be disowned by all true Christians, and let them be reckoned among those base men of the world, which, by such actions, they most resemble. They are Mr. Badman's kindred. For they are a shame to religion, I say, these slithy,[3] rob-shop, pick-pocket men are a shame to religion, and religious men should be ashamed of them. God puts such a person among the fools of the world; therefore, let not Christians put them among those who are wise for heaven. "As the partridge sitteth on eggs and hatcheth them not, so he that getteth riches, and not by right, shall leave them in the midst of his days, and at his end shall be a fool" (Jer. 17:11). And the man under consideration is one of these, and he therefore must look to fall by this judgment.

---

3. *slithy*: slippery, deceitful

A professor! And practice such villainies as these! Such a one is not worthy to bear that name any longer. We may say to such as the prophet spoke to their kind, to wit, to the rebellious who were in the house of Israel: "Go ye, serve ye every one his idols" (Ezek. 20:39). If you will not listen to the law and testament of God to lead your lives, hereafter you will pollute God's holy name no more with your gifts and with your idols.

Go, professors, go; leave off profession, unless you will lead your lives according to your profession. Better never profess than to make profession a stalking horse to sin, deceit, the Devil, and hell. The ground and rules of religion do not allow any such thing: "Receive us," says the apostle, "we have wronged no man, we have corrupted no man, we have defrauded no man" (2 Cor. 7:2). This intimates that those who are guilty of wronging, corrupting, or defrauding of any should not be admitted to the fellowship of saints, no, nor into the common catalog of brothers with them. Nor can men with all their rhetoric and eloquent speaking prove themselves fit for the kingdom of heaven, or men of good conscience on earth. O that godly plea of Samuel: "Behold here I am," he says, "witness against me, before the LORD, and before his anointed: whose ox have I taken? or whose ass have I taken? or whom have I defrauded? whom have I oppressed?" (1 Sam. 12:3). This was to act like a man of good conscience indeed (Matt. 10:19). And in this his appeal, he was so justified in the consciences of the whole congregation that they could not but with one voice, as with one mouth,

Warning to False Professors of Religion 185

break out jointly and say, "Thou hast not defrauded us, nor oppressed us" (Matt. 10:4).

A professor, and defraud—away with him! A professor should not owe any man anything but love. A professor should provide things not of other men's, but of his own, of his own honest getting, and that not only in the sight of God, but of all men; that he may adorn the doctrine of God our Savior in all things.

31

Without Godly Repentance, the Wicked Man's Hope and Life Die Together

For this reason, wicked men's hope is said to die, not before, but with them; they give up the ghost together. And thus did Mr. Badman. His sins and his hope went with him to the gate of death, but there his hope left him, because he died there, but his sins went in with him, to be a worm to gnaw him in conscience forever and ever.

The opinion, therefore, of the common people concerning this kind of dying is frivolous and vain, for Mr. Badman died like a lamb or, as they call it, like a chrisom-child,[1] quietly and without fear. I do not say with reference to the struggling of nature with death, but regarding the struggling of the conscience with the judgment of God. I know that nature will struggle with death. I have seen a dog and sheep die hardly. And thus may a wicked man do, because there is an antipathy between nature and death. But even while, even then, when death and nature are struggling for mastery, the soul, the conscience,

---

From *The Life and Death of Mr. Badman*, in *Works*, 3:663–64.

1. A "chrisom child" is a child who dies within a month of his baptism and is buried in his chrisom robe, a white baptismal robe, instead of a shroud.

may be as besotted, as benumbed, as senseless and ignorant of its miserable state as the block or bed on which the sick lies. And thus they may die like a chrisom-child in show, but indeed like one who by the judgment of God is bound over to eternal damnation; and that also by the same judgment is kept from seeing what they are, and whither they are going, till they plunge down among the flames....

For comparing their life with their death, their sinful, cursed lives, with their childlike, lamblike death, they think that all is well, that no damnation is happening to them. Though they lived like devils incarnate, yet they died like harmless ones. There was no whirlwind, no tempest, no band or plague in their death. They died as quietly as the godliest of them all and had as great faith and hope of salvation and would talk as boldly of salvation as if they had assurance of it. But as was their hope in life, so was their death; their hope was without trial, because it was none of God's working, and their death was without molestation, because so was the judgment of God concerning them....

They are bold, by seeing this, to conclude that God either does not or will not take notice of their sins. They "speak wickedly...loftily" (Ps. 73:8). They speak wickedly of sin, for that they make it better than by the Word it is pronounced to be. They speak wickedly concerning oppression that they commend and count it a prudent act. They also speak loftily. "They set their mouth against the heavens.... And they say, How doth God know? and is there knowledge in the Most High?" (Ps. 73:9–11). And all this, so far as I can see, arises in their hearts from the beholding of the quiet and lamblike death of their companions. "Behold these are the ungodly who prosper in the world," that is, by wicked ways; "they increase in riches" (Ps. 73:12).

This, therefore, is a great judgment of God, both upon that man who dies in his sins and also upon his companion who sees him die in such a way. He sins, he dies in his sins, and yet he dies quietly. What will his companion say about this? What judgment should he make about how God will deal with him by beholding the lamblike death of his companion? Be sure he cannot, as from such a sight, say, "Woe to me," for judgment is before him. He cannot gather that sin is a dreadful and a bitter thing by the childlike death of Mr. Badman. But he must rather, if he judges according to what he sees or according to his corrupted reason, conclude with the wicked ones of old, that "every one that doth evil is good in the sight of the LORD, and he delighteth in them; or, Where is the God of judgment?" (Mal. 2:17).

Yes, this is enough to puzzle the wisest man. David himself was put to a stand by beholding the quiet death of ungodly men. "Verily," he says, "I have cleansed my heart in vain, and washed my hands in innocency" (Ps. 73:13). They, to appearance, fare better by far than I: "Their eyes stand out with fatness: they have more than heart could wish. But all the day long have I been plagued, and chastened every morning" (see v. 7). This, I say, made David wonder, and Job and Jeremiah too. But he goes into the sanctuary, and then he understands their end; he could not understand it before. "I went into the sanctuary of God (v. 17)." What place was that? Why,

Without Godly Repentance

there where he might inquire of God, and by Him he resolved of this matter. "*Then*," he says, "understood I their end." Then I saw that Thou hast "set them in slippery places," and that "thou castedst them down to destruction" (v. 18). "Castedst them down," that is, suddenly, or, as the next words say, "As in a moment they are utterly consumed with terrors" (v. 19). These terrors did not seize them on their sick bed, for they had "no bands" in their death. The terrors, therefore, seized them there, where also they are held in them forever. This he found out, I say, but not without great painfulness, grief, and pricking in his reins—so deep, so hard, and so difficult did he find it rightly to come to a determination in this matter.

And, indeed, this is a deep judgment of God towards ungodly sinners; it is enough to stagger a whole world. Only the godly in the world have a sanctuary to go to, where the oracle and Word of God is, by which His judgments and a reason of many of them are made known to and understood by them.

The Order and Causes of Salvation and Damnation

Bunyan made this chart to explain God's work of grace in the believer and the demise of those bound in sin.

Reading Bunyan

Many people are familiar with *Pilgrim's Progress*, but they may not realize that Bunyan produced more than sixty works during his lifetime. We hope that this brief introduction to Bunyan's life and lesser-known writings will spur inquisitive readers to investigate the wide range of literature this persecuted saint left to the church. We commend the following works to you, hoping that by reading them you will gain a fuller appreciation and understanding of Bunyan's life and times.

Works by Bunyan

The Works of John Bunyan, edited by George Offor, was first published in 1854 as a compilation of fifty-five works in three volumes. Banner of Truth Trust reprinted Offor's edition in 1991. Bunyan's allegorical works are the content of volume 3, and his many experiential, doctrinal, and practical works are contained in volumes 1 and 2. Volume 1 also includes an eighty-page memoir of Bunyan's life and times.

Editions of Bunyan's individual writings are readily available as well, and we recommend the following for those who would like to sample some of the best of this prolific author's works.

The Acceptable Sacrifice. The final work Bunyan prepared for publication, this moving exposition of Psalm 51:17 considers the necessity of a broken and contrite heart before God.

Grace Abounding to the Chief of Sinners. In his autobiography, Bunyan writes about his life, from infancy to his imprisonment in 1660, chronicling his struggles and his conversion.

The Holy War. This dramatic allegory is more challenging reading than *Pilgrim's Progress*, but it is also more profound. Written after his imprisonment, Bunyan's work portrays the spiritual warfare between Christ and Satan for the town of Mansoul and God's final triumph over sin and evil. Some Bunyan scholars consider this his second greatest work.

The Jerusalem Sinner Saved. Out of a sense of his own sinfulness and in recognition of God's mercy and grace to him, Bunyan published this volume in the year of his death so that, as he explained, his companions in sin could partake of God's mercy and forgiveness as well.

The Life and Death of Mr. Badman. Considered by many to be an early novel, this work was published between the two parts of *Pilgrim's Progress* in 1680 as a companion story. Just as *Pilgrim's Progress* follows Christian's journey from this world to glory, *The Life and Death of Mr. Badman* traces the journey of the ungodly through this world to perdition.

The Pilgrim's Progress. Written at least in part during Bunyan's imprisonment, this famous classic allegory traces the journey that Christian and others make from the City of Destruction to the Celestial City. There have been many versions of *Pilgrim's Progress* retold for children, among them *Dangerous Journey: The Story of Pilgrim's Progress* (text by Oliver Hunkin and illustrations by Alan Perry, Eerdmans, 1985), a shortened version that remains faithful to Bunyan's original story.

Works about Bunyan

Calhoun, David B. *Grace Abounding: The Life, Books and Influence of John Bunyan*. Fearn, Scotland: Christian Focus Publications, 2005. Calhoun writes about Bunyan's life and analyzes his books, theology, and place in history and includes summaries of several of his major works. The author provides an annotated bibliography for further Bunyan studies as well.

Cook, Faith. *Fearless Pilgrim: The Life and Times of John Bunyan*. Darlington, U.K.: Evangelical Press, 2008. Christian biographer Cook provides a new, well-written biography that chronicles the life and times of Bunyan.

Cosby, Brian H. *John Bunyan: The Journey of a Pilgrim*. Fearn, Scotland: Christian Focus, 2009. Cosby's biography, part of the Trail Blazers series, traces the events of Bunyan's life and the development of his theology for children.

Horner, Barry E. *Pilgrim's Progress: Themes and Issues.* Vestavia Hills, Ala.: Solid Ground Christian Books, 2003. Horner considers the major themes running through the allegory and asserts its relevance for twenty-first-century readers.

Pestell, John. *Travel with John Bunyan.* Surrey, U.K.: Day One, 2002. This compact book is both a biography and a travel guide that contains over a hundred color photographs and maps of the key locations associated with Bunyan.